Naughty Games for Lovers

50 sealed, sexual games for lovers,
each one guaranteed to tease and tantalize
the hungriest sexual appetites.

Tear out pages to reveal one hot
"sexcapade" after another!!

A must for lovers everywhere!!!

Compiled from
stories and suggestions
contributed by lovers nationwide

Edited By:
Alex and Elizabeth Lluch

Published by WS Publishing

Printed in China

ISBN 1-887169-08-3

DISCLAIMER- PLEASE READ BEFORE OPENING GAMES

This book is sold with the knowledge that its intent is solely for consenting adults in their pursuit of sexual fulfillment. Readers are hereby advised that each of the games contained in this book is completely voluntary and to be played at the readers' own risk.

Neither the publisher nor the editors assume any responsibility to any person for any damage or losses caused or allegedly caused, indirectly or directly, by participating in the scenarios contained in this book.

If you do not agree with the above disclaimer, you may return the book, with all the games unopened, for a full refund of the purchase price to: WS Publishing, 6347 Caminito Tenedor, San Diego, California, 92120.

Introduction

Naughty Games for Lovers is the second in a series of books written for men and women who are wanting to add some spice to their sexual lives. Whether you are young and a bit inexperienced, older and caught in a routine, in a new relationship or have been together for years, Naughty Games for Lovers is for you.

Are you ready to make your sex life sizzle? This book contains 50 sealed pages - 25 for the woman to pleasure her lover and 25 for the man to pleasure his lover. A heart icon at the bottom of each page indicates whether the game is to be selected by the man or the woman. Let the titles titillate your senses and your imagination and then tear open the sealed page to reveal the day's (or night's) romantically seductive events. Take turns choosing one of these special adventures and get ready to enjoy new ways of kindling or rekindling the flames of desire for one another.

Naughty Games for Lovers contains a wide variety of experiences to share with your mate. Use these encounters to add some extra lust to your love life. Some of the games may make you feel as if you are taking a "walk on the wild side." It's natural to have some hesitations about trying something daring and new, but that is exactly why you are holding this book in your hand! Test your sense of adventure and have some fun exploring different ways of arousing and satisfying one another. Get wet and wild, frisky and free! Most of all, have FUN!

Your reward for playing Naughty Games for Lovers? Spicy, steamy, sizzling sex and a new found passion for that special someone in your life! What are you waiting for?

Table Of Contents

Naughty Game

#1

Dance Of The Seven Veils

Turn him into your Arabian Night!

Dance Of The Seven Veils

One of the most erotic images for a man is that of a woman sensuously swaying her body to the rhythm of sexy music as she slowly teases him with the unveiling of her form. Instead of sending him off with the boys for an occasional night on the town or to a bachelor party complete with strippers, tonight you are going to fulfill his every fantasy.

There are very simple props you need to accomplish your mission. A sexy, lacy bra and matching panties or a thong will do nicely. Then, to add drama and mystery, you will drape yourself artfully with seven different scarves - veils, if you will - to perform the ancient ritual: Dance Of The Seven Veils!

Select music that has a slow beat and soft, moody sounds. Some women who are a bit bashful, even with their lifelong lover, find it helpful to sip a glass of wine prior to their performance. Dimming the lights will overcome any reticence you may have, as well as help set the mood. And lastly, fill the room with the musky aroma of incense.

When you enter the room, step gracefully and proudly, with your head held high. This simple act of confidence will help bolster your sense of assurance while stimulating his desire. Listen to the music for a moment, until you feel it in your soul and can begin moving to its rhythm. Reach for the first scarf and tug it free from your body as you turn and let it flow over your head and around your curves. Continue in the same way until each scarf has been removed, always creating an aura of sexual arousal with each twist and turn. As you sway in your skimpiest under things, standing amidst a pile of sheer and colorful scarves, his lust will be visible.

Go to him - NOW! No man can resist the power of a woman, especially the one he loves, when she has given of herself by performing the Dance Of The Seven Veils.

Nicknames for Her

Mount of Venus
Nectar Unit
Candy Box
Pot O' Gold
Big Boy's Joy

Naughty Game

#2

Viva Las Vegas

Take a trip to the Strip!

Viva Las Vegas

While you might not be able to plan a getaway to the fabulous city of Las Vegas, you can certainly recreate one of the draws this city is famous for - that of lusty ladies dancing topless to please an audience. Most cities offer nightclubs designed to please and titillate couples looking to add a little thrill to their ordinary lives. Play this game with the spirit of being transported to Viva Las Vegas!

Start the evening with a special dinner at one of her favorite restaurants. You may need to do a little confidence building as a prelude to this game, and your thoughtfulness of a dinner location will assure her that your primary focus is her pleasure. Make her feel special by holding her chair and ordering for her. Share a bit of your own meal with her, tempting her with a morsel from your own fork. Reach across the table to gently wipe the edges of her mouth with your thumb, then inserting your thumb into your own mouth, sucking it clean, then sensuously licking your lips. Escort her to the car afterward, open her door and tell her you have a surprise "nightcap" for the evening.

When you arrive at the nightclub of your choice, be sure to ease her entry into this sexual encounter with verbal assurances of your attraction for her. Let her know that this game is intended for her pleasure. When you enter the club, have your arm around her, caressing her shoulder, letting your hand slip down to her breast. As you guide her toward a table, fondle her butt as you help her into her chair. Urge her to keep her eyes on the show, as you keep your eyes hungrily on her, with only the subtlest glimpse toward the performers. Watch for her reactions, while you let your hands roam across her legs, slipping their way up under her dress to find a wet and waiting pussy. Whisper into her ear your thoughts of what you will do to her once you get home. As she watches the show, and you watch her, the two of you will soon be unable to keep your hands to yourselves, and will be rushing home to live out your fantasies of Viva Las Vegas!

Nicknames for Him

Purple Helmet
Soldier of Love
Hard Drive
Mr. Happy
Tube Steak

Naughty Game

#3

Turn Up The Heat

Alert the Fire Department before you begin!

Turn Up The Heat

Want to make your man sizzle with desire? Tonight's game starts with a hot, flaming fire in your fireplace and has you stoking the fire in his loins as you Turn Up The Heat with tricks of your own.

Begin by building a warm, cozy fire this evening. Lay a comforter on the floor in front of the fireplace and arrange several pillows for your lounging comfort. Enjoy the ambiance for awhile, sip some wine, listen to soft music as you both unwind from a long day. Feel the stresses seep away, freeing you both to enjoy the activities to come.

Slip away to the bedroom and return with two of your lover's ties or the sash from your bathrobe. Stand over your man as you dangle the ties above his head. Bend down and gently wrap one end of a tie around his wrist and secure the other end to a leg of your coffee table. Repeat the procedure with his other wrist, so that you have him firmly anchored. If you like, bind his ankles together too, rendering him powerless and unable to resist your further advances. His excitement at your display of power will become evident, growing harder, bulging beneath his clothes. Add another log to the fire, as you continue to Turn Up The Heat.

Remove your shirt, but not your bra. Instead, slip the cups of your bra down underneath your breasts, forcing them upward and outward. Let him watch you play with your nipples, making them hard and inviting. Continue to strip away the rest of your clothes, watching the heat rising in his face, his body as he squirms and pulls against his restraints. Dangle your tits over his mouth, teasing him, pulling away just out of his reach. Unbutton and unzip his pants, pulling them down just to his knees, and catch his cock in your hands as it bursts free from its prison. Stroke him, as you stoked the fire. Turn Up The Heat until you are ready to douse the flames by easing your wet pussy down over his dick, encasing his fire and letting it spit forth into your waiting vessel.

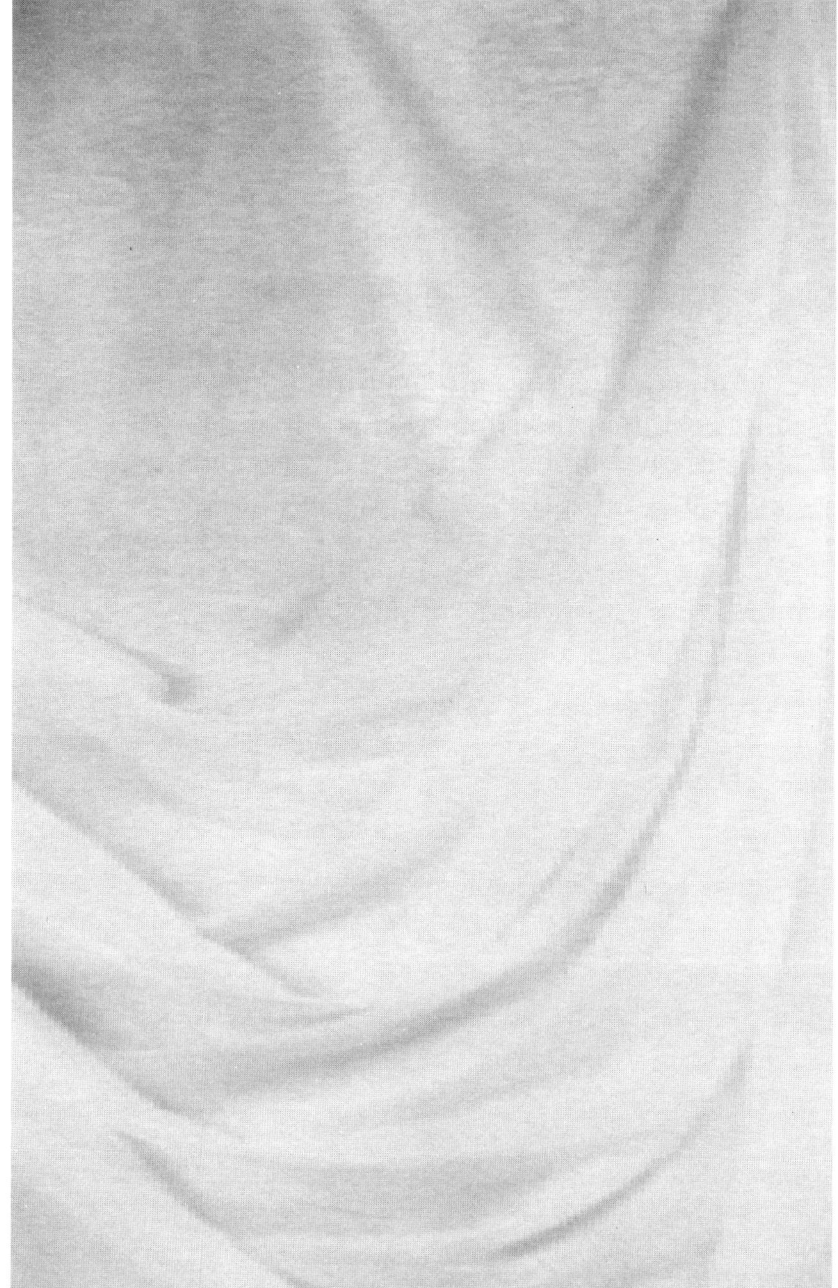

Kissing Turn-Ons

Both men and women equally are turned on by French kissing, as well as kissing in public. Women, however, enjoy a little playful biting more so than their mates. Ear nibbling? Twice as many women as men find it makes them hot. But the biggest difference is their response to neck kissing: women outnumber men 10 to 1 favoring neck licks as their prelude to passion.

Naughty Game

#4

Variety Is The Spice Of Life

A hot night may be in the cards tonight!

Variety Is The Spice Of Life

When you were a child, do you remember how short your attention span was? There was a thrill to running from one thing to the next, pausing just long enough to extract a few moments of pleasure before trying something new. Tonight you're going to recapture that thrill of a time when you knew in your heart that Variety Is The Spice Of Life!

To prepare to play, you need 30, 3 x 5 inch blank index cards and a kitchen timer. On the first 10 cards, write 10 different home locations you've never experimented with when making love. Look around the house and the yard. What about the dryer, the kitchen floor, the dining room table, the hall closet, a recliner in the family room? Have you ever done it on a lounge chair on the patio, a hammock hanging from the trees, on the work bench in the garage, in the hot tub, or on the front porch swing?

After you have chosen the locations, you're next going to choose 10 different lengths of time to write on the next set of cards. Keep them on the short side, ranging between 5 and 20 minutes.

Last, but not least, you'll write these five sexual positions (missionary position; doggy style; 69; her on top, riding the pony express; standing up) and these five "zones" of the body (neck and up; arms and chest; belly and back; groin and buttocks; legs and toes).

The rules of the game are simple. You'll shuffle each of the three sets of cards, placing them alongside each other. Taking turns, you and your lady will draw one card from each set then go to the chosen location, setting a timer for the prescribed length of time. If you've chosen a sexual position, it is the one you'll perform. If you chose one of the five "zones", you will spend your allotted time concentrating on touching, kissing, licking, sucking, just that area of your lover. When the timer rings, it's on to the next pick of the cards, rekindling the fun of sampling one thing after another, in a game of Variety - The Spice Of Life!

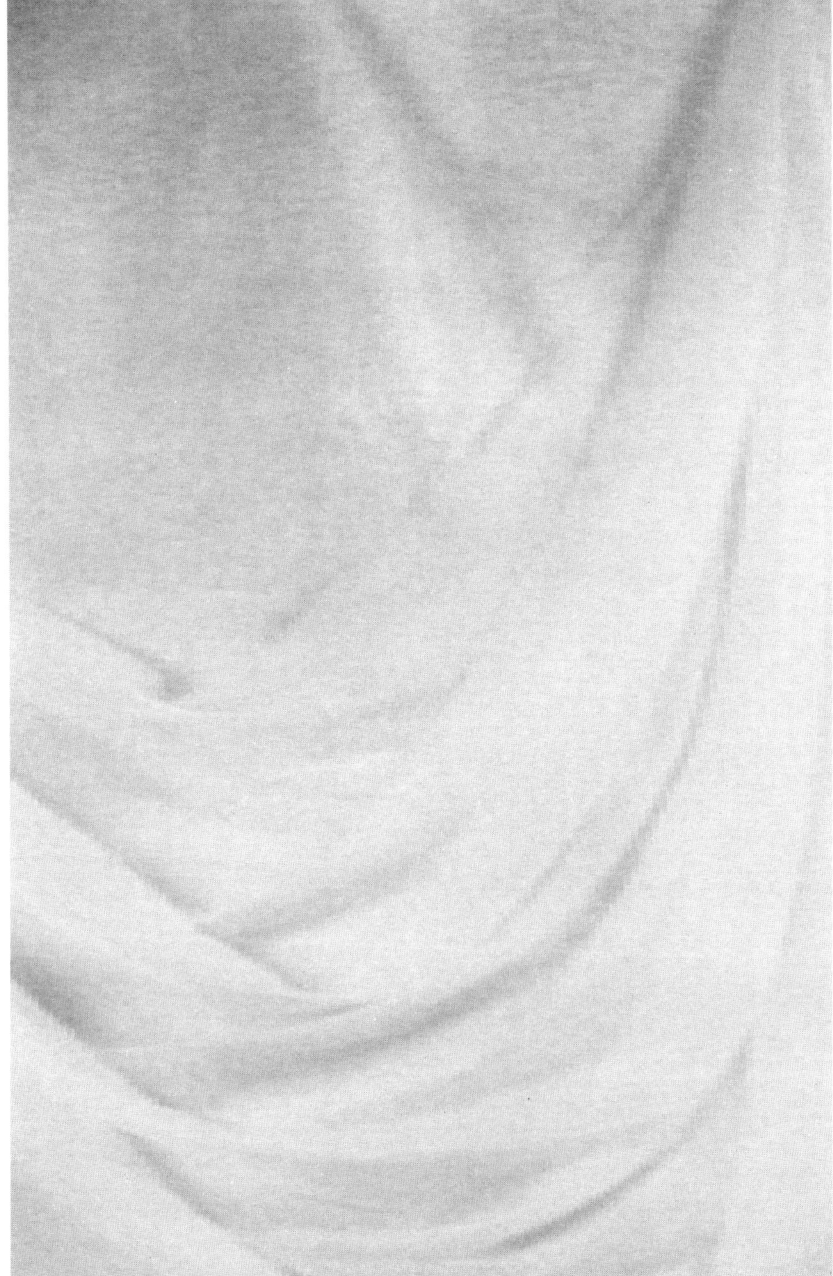

Bring Back the Romance

Cover your bed with rose petals
Send a singing telegram
Give love coupons
Watch the sunrise or sunset, with
champagne and strawberries
Leave the dishes ’til tomorrow

Naughty Game

#5

Coffee, Tea...Or Me?

Breakfast of Champions...

Coffee, Tea...Or Me?

While breakfast in bed is usually a treat more desired by women, sometimes the best way to teach your man what YOU like is to show him how sweet it can be! Men can only learn to pamper when they have been pampered themselves. Besides, you are going to sweeten the pot by serving him more than just bacon and eggs in bed. He won't have much trouble making a choice when he's offered Coffee, Tea...Or Me!

Plan to play this game on a morning when you both can lounge (and romp and tussle and tease) leisurely in bed. Arise early to cook his favorite breakfast (although you could serve him burned toast or dry cereal and he wouldn't even notice.) Arrange the food attractively on a bed tray, place a single flower in a bud vase, and include a cloth napkin. For the finishing touch, strip yourself naked, then wrap a cloth tablecloth around yourself.

Knock before you enter the bedroom, to get his attention, then sashay into the room with a flourish and place the tray on the bureau. Turn to face him and announce, "Honey, I thought you'd enjoy a special treat this morning. Would you like Coffee, Tea...Or Me?" With that, pull the tablecloth from around your bare self, shake it out and place it over his lap. He'll be scrambling to sit up with all parts of his mind and body arousing at the sight of you. Carry the tray to the bed, place it in front of him and straddle his legs revealing part of the breakfast menu. Using your fingers, slip a morsel of food between his lips, then feed yourself a bite as well. Licking your fingers clean, making them moist, let them slip between your legs to explore your own hot oven. Cup a breast in your hand, lean forward and offer him a taste of your goods. Pull away the sheets and savor his ripe banana. Coffee, Tea...Or Me? His choice will be all too clear. The traditional breakfast will be quickly cast aside as he reaches out for the sustenance that revs his engines, morning, noon, or night.

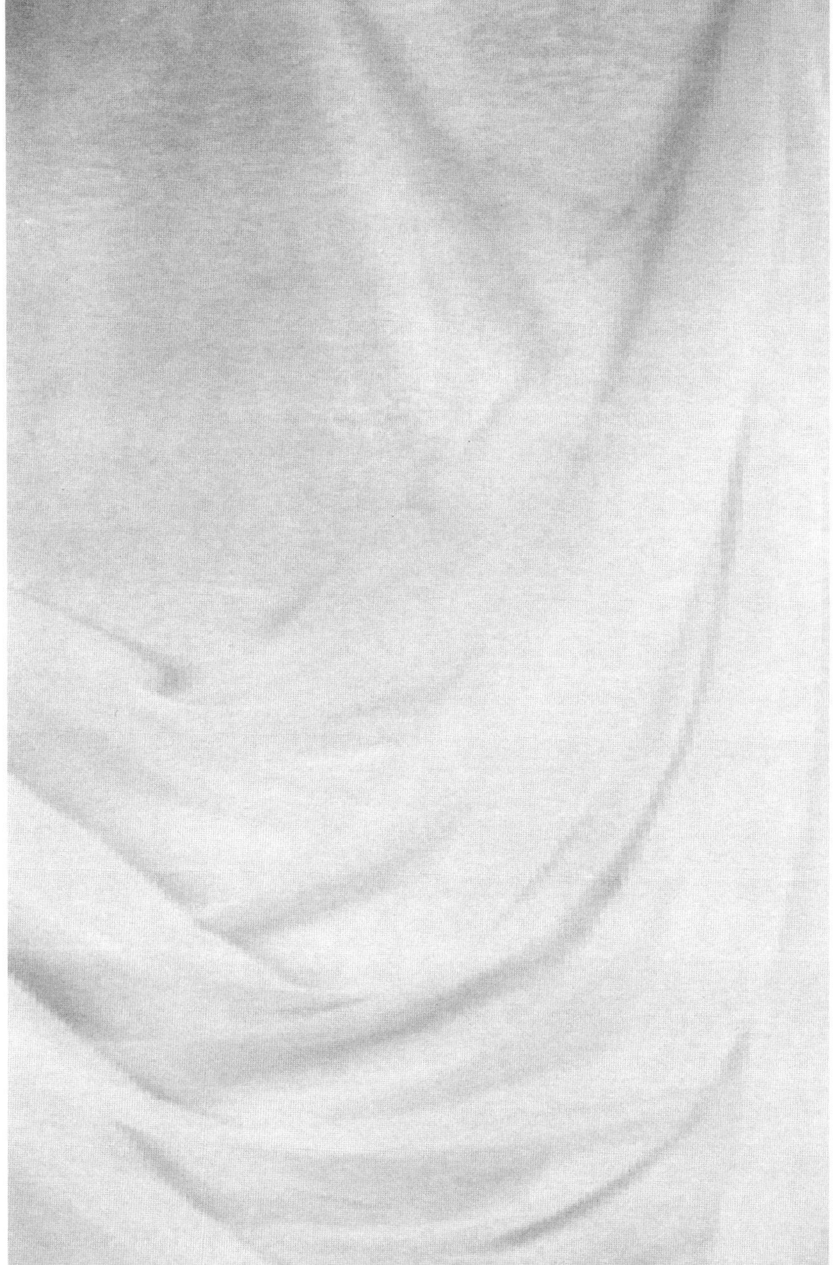

Gadgets for the Adventurous Female
(For him to use on her!)

Nipple Clamps
Ben Wa Balls
Clit Clips
Remote Control Vibrator
Riding Crop

Naughty Game

#6

Wait And See

A gift a day
keeps the boredom away!

Wait and See

Women love to be showered with gifts - especially when they aren't tied to a certain occasion such as their anniversary, their birthday or a holiday. Starting on Monday, then for six days in a row, you are going to send your lover a wrapped gift, along with a note each day that simply says, "Save this till Sunday, then Wait and See."

On day one, send her a pair of gloves. Depending on your preference, you may choose a short, lacy pair or perhaps the ones that reach just past her elbow. If you are unsure where to make such a purchase, try one of the accessory shops found in most malls.

For day two, select a sexy garter belt for your partner to wear. Day three should then be a pair of stockings. There are so many varieties to choose from - you may want sheer stockings with a seam up the back, ones with a design, or perhaps some kinky fishnet ones!

Days four and five you'll be accessorizing the top of her body. Be daring, encouraging her to be as well, when you select either a half-cup bra that lifts her breasts while exposing the nipples or a cut-out bra that lets her sweet nips poke through the center. The other gift should be some jewelry - try either a choker to accentuate her delicate neck or a very long string of fake pearls.

The last gift can be as simple as her favorite bottle of wine, or perhaps you'll splurge on some champagne with elegant flutes engraved with your names.

Be imaginative with your delivery process. Use a courier to deliver one or more gifts to her workplace; have one of her girlfriends assist you in the surprise; or leave them daily in different spots in the house - on her pillow, in the bathroom next to her makeup, or tucked in her lingerie drawer. By the seventh day, her curiosity will be satisfied having all the props necessary for a fun romp of sexual delights with the man she loves - the one who teased her, pampered her all week with gifts in a game of Wait and See.

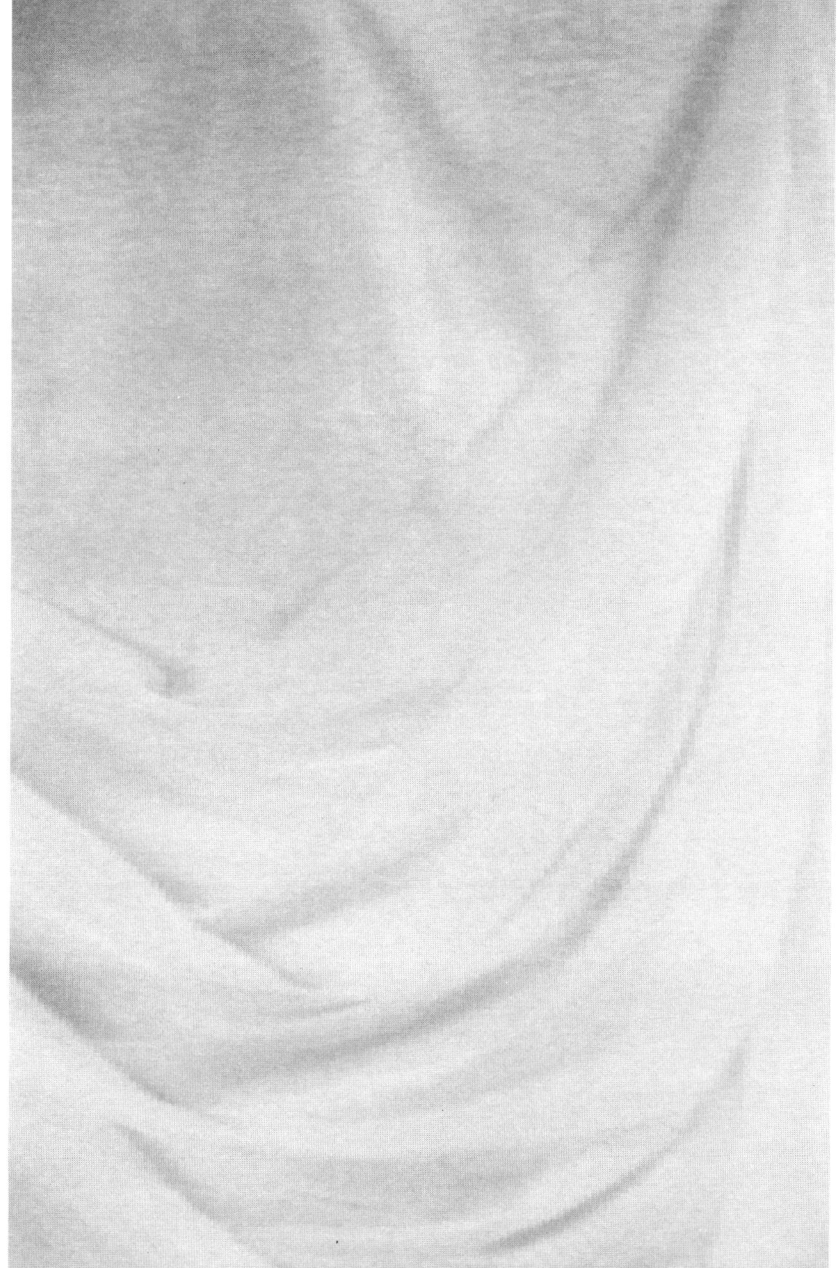

Gadgets for the Adventurous Male
(For her to use on him!)

Cock Ring
Penis Pump
Harness
Anal Plug
Edible Gel

Naughty Game

#7

Picture This!

Has he been working late?
Not tonight!

Picture This!

Is your man someone who enjoys the stimulation of looking at erotic poses of men and women together? Does he become aroused, and get new ideas when he can visualize the different ways in which couples touch each other, lick private parts, probe tongue or fingers or a stiff cock into various openings? Would you like to take some control and be the one to invite him to try something new? Then Picture This is the game to get you started!

Pick up several of the magazines available for couples - not the ones that focus just on a woman alone, or a man alone. Or visit the bookstore where you will easily find a wide variety of pictorial guides that demonstrate numerous positions for experimental lovemaking. Find a position that excites you, something different from anything the two of you have ever tried before. Maybe it will show a man lying on his back with his woman sitting on top of him facing backward. Or a man standing, firmly supporting his lover by her buttocks as she has her legs wrapped around his waist. Or she may be standing, bent forward at the waist as if touching her toes and he is entering her from behind. Just make sure your choice is unusual to the two of you, and something you both are physically capable of.

Make a copy of the picture, or tear the page from the book or magazine and send it to your lover at work. Enclose a perfumed note that says, "Picture This! You and me ... tonight! Can't wait!"

Expect your honey home a little earlier than usual, as his senses will be reeling after receiving such an invitation. Plan a simple snack for later - you won't have time to cook a meal, much less eat one. His flagpole will be at attention when he walks through the door, because he will have spent all day smelling your perfume and picturing the two of you trying something new, something you cooked up with his pleasure in mind!

Herbal Aphrodisiacs

(Consult your doctor first!)

Damiana - a sexual stimulant
Saw Palmetto - increases libido
Ginseng - increases stamina
Chinese Angelica - an overall sexual stimulant

Naughty Game

#8

Kidnap!

She'll be bound
to pay this ransom!

Kidnap!

Many women long for their lover to take the initiative to plan and execute an exciting surprise. Your effort alone is indeed an aphrodisiac. It shows that you care, that you are interested in adding some spice to your normal routines and ultimately your relationship. You are going to win big points when you plan to Kidnap her for a day of fun.

You will need to make a few advance plans to pull this off. Enlist the help of some of her co-workers. Tell them your plan, so they can help with the arrangements. They will be envious of your ingenuity and will be delighted to play a part in the whole scheme. You may decide to Kidnap her for an entire day, just the afternoon, or immediately after work, depending upon the flexibility you both have at your jobs.

Make reservations at a hotel for the escapade. Pack a bag of bare necessities for her - perhaps this is the time to splurge and buy her some sexy little outfit. She won't need or want anything else! Plan for a meal for your hostage, to give her sustenance for the night ahead! A picnic basket filled with snacks and wine for an interlude at the park or a cooler to take into the room will keep you both energized without having to interrupt the purpose of the evening.

At the chosen hour, intercept your sweetheart during a routine activity such as locking her car to go into the office or heading out for lunch with her friends. Tell her she is being Kidnapped and will be held without ransom till the following morning! You'll be able to whisk her away, stunned, caught up in the excitement of the drama. For added effect, tie her hands behind her back, gag her, and even blindfold her as you capture her body and soul for this adventure. Take her to your rented room, and shove her gently onto the bed, letting her know that your passion for her is too great to contain. Rip away her clothes and ravage her body. Her thrill at your impetuousness will heighten all her senses, carrying her into a sexual frenzy of playing the victim in your Kidnap scheme!

Masturbation Nicknames

Spank the Monkey
Polish the Pearl
Make a Milkshake
Unbutton the Fur Coat
Playing Pocket Pool
Petting the Bunny
Fingerpainting
Sex With Someone You Love
Choke the Chicken
Roughing Up the Suspect

Naughty Game

#9

The Cheerleader

Score the winning goal!

The Cheerleader

Tonight you are going to recreate some of the nostalgia of being young and in love, sneaking away from the crowds to play naughty, but nice!

To set the stage, first arrange to borrow or rent a classic convertible. Select some tapes or CD's of your favorite "oldies but goodies," the songs that will remind you both of your youth. The role you'll be playing is of the beautiful, popular Cheerleader, while he will become the Captain of the football team. Prepare your outfit - a short, pleated shirt or shorts, a tight sweater, anklets and tennis shoes, and your hair in a ponytail. Bring along a pair of jeans and a football jersey for your lover. Purchase tickets to a local sporting event, one that will get your both all steamed up by watching a field of powerful players engaged in physical competition, and the intensity of a cheering crowd.

Plan to pick your man up at work. His interest will be piqued just by the sight of you. Ask him to drive, but sit as close to him as you can, running your fingers through his hair, down his arm and between his legs, as you nuzzle his neck. While his hunger for you is growing, suggest a quick stop before the game for a bite to eat. What was your favorite food back then? Burgers and fries, pizza, or a hot fudge sundae? In any case, the real dessert will come later!

As you are enjoying the game, keep the momentum going of surprises to come. Dare to show your affection publicly, like you did when you were 16. Throw your arms around him when your team scores a goal. Jump up and down, letting him admire your bouncy tits. Sneak a kiss, cop a feel - be frisky and free! For the best is yet to be!

After the game when the crowd has cleared, grab his hand and lead him back out to the parking lot to your car, teenagers again. Glance at your watch and tell him you have time for a quickie before your curfew. He'll be ripe and ready to score that final goal, and you'll have him saying "rah, rah, rah" all the way home with his favorite Cheerleader.

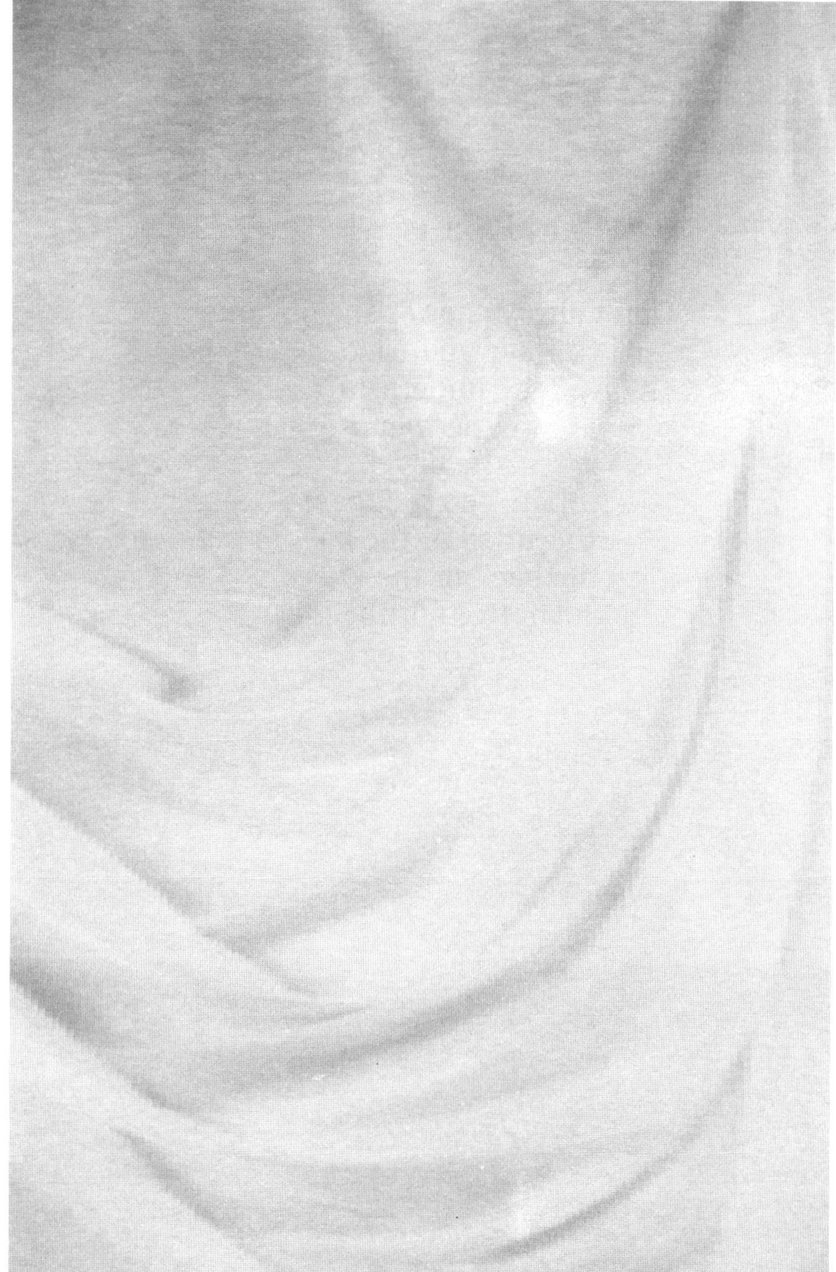

Put My Lips Where?

Don't always go for the obvious!
Have you tried...
the underarm?
the perineum?
the navel?
between the toes?
the small of the back?
the back of the knees?
the bottom of the feet?
the big toe?

Naughty Game

#10

Kinky Kalling Kard

Dial "S" for Sex!

Kinky Kalling Kard

One of your hottest fantasies is bound to be a threesome, yet not one of you is likely to act out with the woman you love. As in all aspects of a relationship, though, you'll find that a little compromise can go a long way. Giving your lover a **Kinky Kalling Kard** for phone sex between the two of you and another woman can tease and please you while protecting your lover's needs for safety and security.

Undoubtedly you have seen 900 phone numbers advertised in a variety of places - on television or in magazines. Many 900 numbers advertise some type of "specialty", including oral fantasies, party lines, domination, or self masturbation. There is something for everyone, so first you must find and select one that appeals to you and will excite your lover as well. Write the phone number on an index card, with the heading "**Kinky Kalling Kard.**"

Your next, and most important step, is to get her in the mood. For a woman to feel adventurous, to be willing to experiment with something new, especially something she may find a bit threatening on some level, you need to prepare her. Before you present her with the card, spend some time cuddling, fondling, and kissing her, thus arousing her desire. Be verbal. Tell her how much she excites you, how beautiful her body is, how much you want to touch it and make it yours. Tell her you want to try something new - together. As long as she sees this as an activity to arouse her too, your joint pleasure will make her a willing partner.

Give her the card and talk about what direction you both want the phone call to take. Once you place the call, (a speaker phone is helpful), tell them what you want. A good beginning to **Kinky Kalling** is to have them describe to you both how and where to touch each other. As the call goes on, you may want to direct the call toward pretending that the other woman is touching one or both of you. Whatever is said, you are both in control, all the while sharing new avenues of excitement.

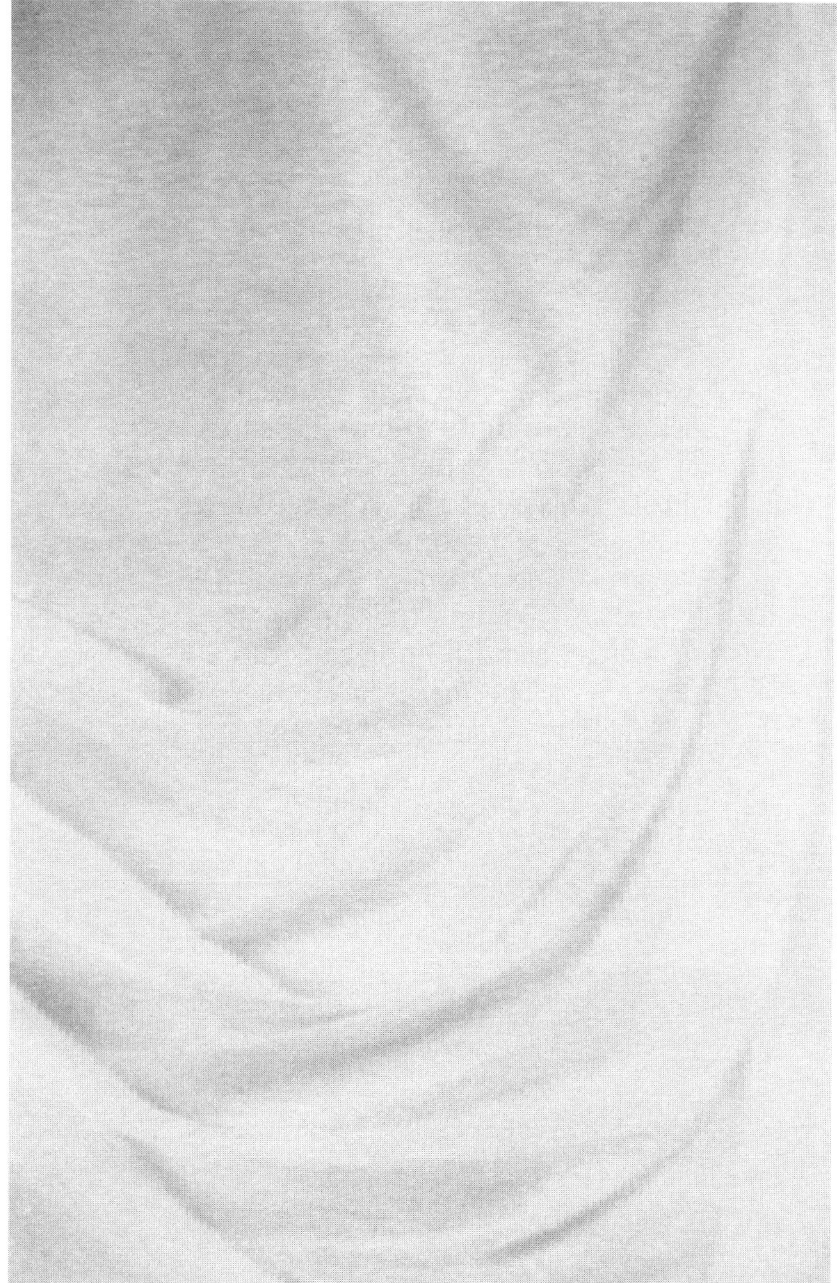

Stock Your Library

The Kama Sutra
Nudes
The Erotic Lives of Women
The Claiming of Sleeping Beauty
Secret Sexual Positions
Erotic Massage: The Touch of Love
Passion Play
The Ultimate Kiss
Awakening the Virgin
The Mammoth Book of Erotica
The Joy of Sex
The Sensuous Woman

Naughty Game

#11

Home Movies

Direct and produce his pleasure!

Home Movies

This Home Movies game is intended to use a variety of sexually arousing stimuli, resulting in one of the hottest nights you've ever had together! You'll need a video camera to capture some erotic images of you inviting your lover to play. You're going to send it to him at his workplace, to heighten the anticipation of what's to come. And you're going to plan a surprise finale to complete the experience!

Step one in this game is to beg, borrow, or rent a video camera and tripod, so that you can film yourself doing a strip tease. With steamy music in the background, capture several minutes of yourself on film. Wear some sexy lingerie - remember red is the color of passion - and strip your way down until you are nude from the waist up. To build the anticipation, remember to wear gloves that you can strip off one at a time, and a coat or dress that you can ease off your shoulders and let slip to the floor before you step out of it and toss it aside. The last footage of your Home Movie should be of you letting your breasts burst forth from your lingerie top. Cross your arms over your tits and say, "To be continued," then halt the camera!

Step two is to send this video to your lover at work with a note that says, "Watch this! Want this? Come home!"

Step three, the surprise finale, has you lying in wait for your very excited man to arrive home. Hide - in a closet or in the bathroom - until you hear him urgently calling your name. Be dressed <u>exactly</u> as you were in the last scene of the Home Movie you sent, and be ready to cue the music before you step forth to assume the last position you were holding in the film - your arms over your tits. Be ready to continue with the final dance of seduction. Complete your strip tease, taking your time to rebuild his excitement. Caress your nipples, tweak them, and wink at him. Let your own hands roam your body as you remove the rest of your lingerie. He'll play, because you'll have him in the palm of your hand with your very own Home Movies!

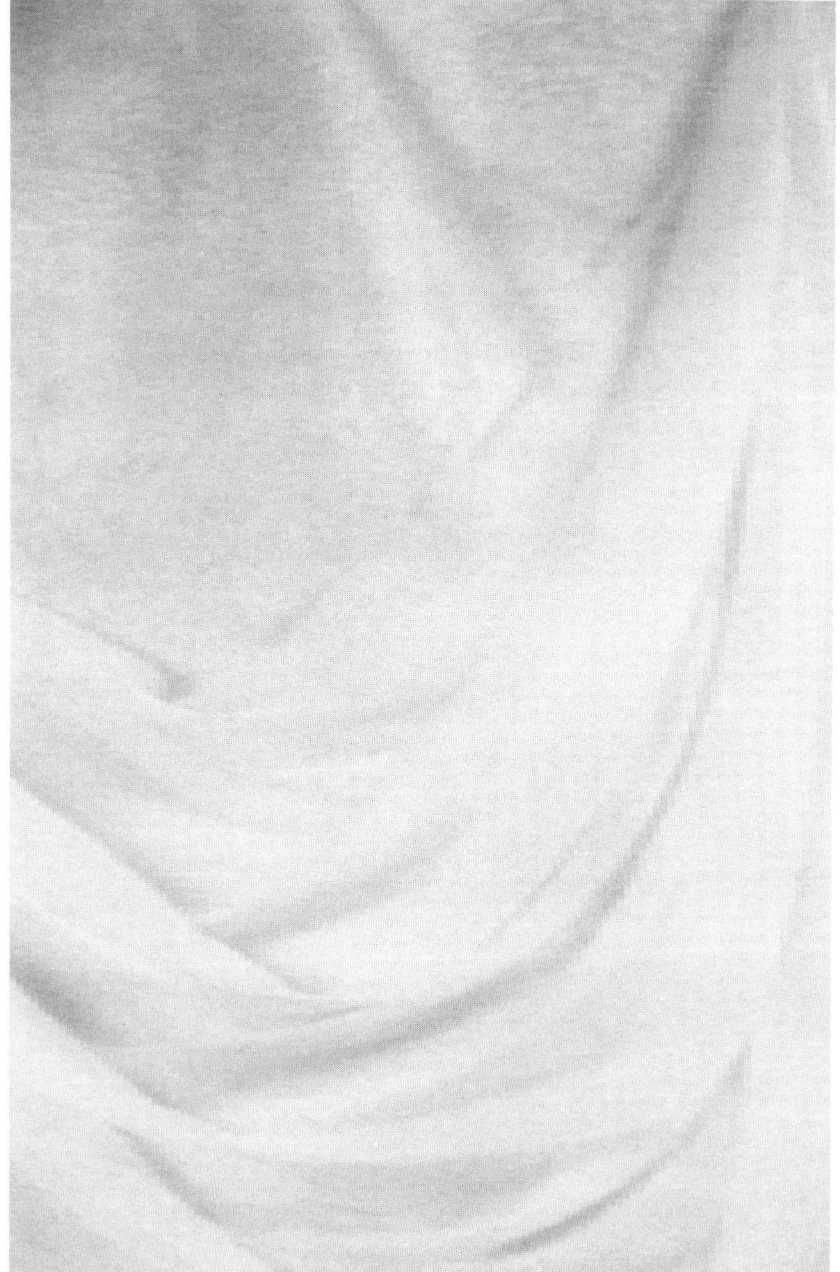

A Simple Secret

Locking eyes with a lover is the most intimate act you can perform when making love.

Naughty Game #12

Magic Fingers

Give me your tired,
your poor,
your oiled muscles...

Magic Fingers

Women love to be pampered. Given the chance, your sweetheart would love to be at the beauty salon having a manicure or pedicure, letting someone else wash her hair or give her a facial. And to a woman, one of the most extravagant forms of pampering is getting a massage.

Even the most professional massage is an erotic experience. Lights are dim and soft music drifts through the air combined with the sweet essence of the oils used to smooth and soften the skin. With her eyes closed, Magic Fingers touch and knead and caress every inch of her body. Her mind can float into a never-never land of thoughts and images of sexual interludes. What if his hands were to slip and brush against her taut nipples? Or move so high upon her thigh that they felt the moisture of her longing? With a professional massage, her fantasies will remain just that. But with this game, they will become a reality!

You are going to arrange for a professional masseuse to come to your home to give your woman one hour of intensely deep, relaxing massage. And you are going to watch, observing his technique and her pleasure. When the hour is over, and he has left your home, you are going to take over where he left off, bringing her to new heights of desire.

Your own Magic Fingers will not have to be as masterfully trained as his, because you will have the advantage of touching her far more deeply than he. Your fingers will slip between her waiting "lips" to caress the pleasure knob found hidden inside. Your fingers, well oiled, will ease their way between the cheeks of her buttocks. They will travel north to squeeze and flick her tits, creating moans of delight as she writhes in pleasure. Finally you will offer her your largest Magic Finger, well oiled and powerful, ready to massage her tightest muscle, as you plunge deep within her for a total body relaxation finale.

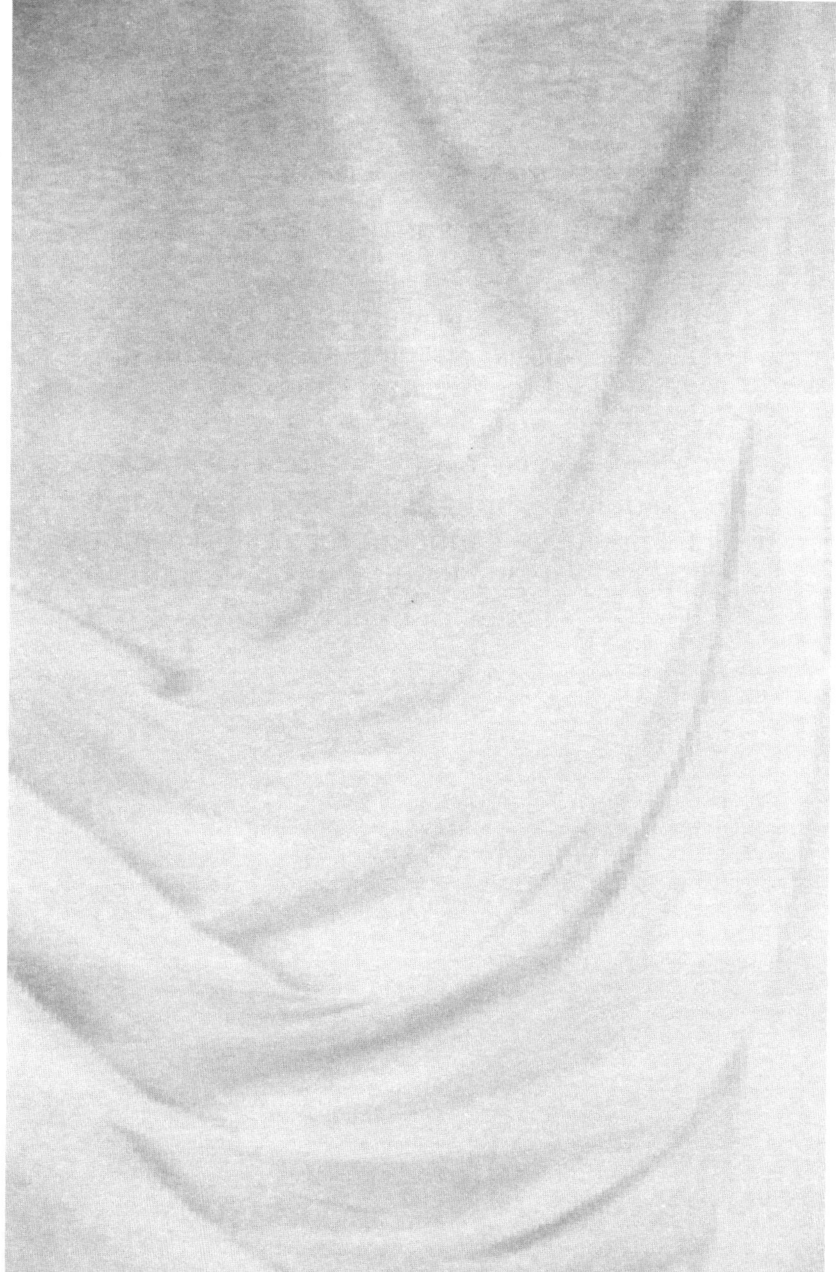

How Does Passion Rate?

78% of men and 74% of women surveyed name passion as the #1 essential element for a healthy, long-term relationship.

Think you've lost it? There's hope! Most people are optimistic - 68% of men and 86% of women are confident they can recapture it! They're probably holding this book in their hands right now!

Naughty Game

#13

Magnificent Mistress

You'll have him eating out of your. . . hand!

Magnificent Mistress

Despite the changing times, men often feel the pressures of taking the lead in the business world, as well as taking the lead at home, particularly in the bedroom. Every so often, a man likes to turn over that lead, surrender some of his control, and have his woman take charge. Tonight you are going to rise to the occasion and seize the opportunity of becoming his dominatrix, his Magnificent Mistress.

Sleek, strong, commanding - these are your cues. In order to play the role effectively, creating a visual image to match your new personality, you must dress for success in stark, simple style. Your entire outfit will consist of nothing more than sheer black thigh-high stockings, four-inch black high heels, a black leather belt around your waist and one of his darkest ties knotted at your neck.

When he arrives home for the evening, you must be ready to confidently assert your authority over him. Stand at the doorway of your bedroom, feet spread, arms crossed under your naked tits, lifting them high and mighty. Without saying a word, swivel to one side to let him pass, turning to swat him on his backside as he enters the room. Give him a shove toward the bed, then position yourself directly in front of him, hands on your hips, as you spit out just one word - "Strip!" With long strides, pace back and forth before him as he meekly complies with your demand. If he starts to approach you, order him back to the bed with a terse, "Sit!" Once he is completely naked, loosen and remove the tie from your neck, wrapping it around his wrists and forcing him to stand. The sheer intensity of watching you, being dominated by his Magnificent Mistress, will be firmly evident in his uncontrollably swollen cock. Next remove your belt, snapping it as a whip in the space beside you. Move toward him and with just one index finger push him back down on the bed as you lash the belt around his ankles to restrain him further. As you force your wet cunt down over his staff, let him know, "It's my turn to seize and plunder what I want - and I want YOU!"

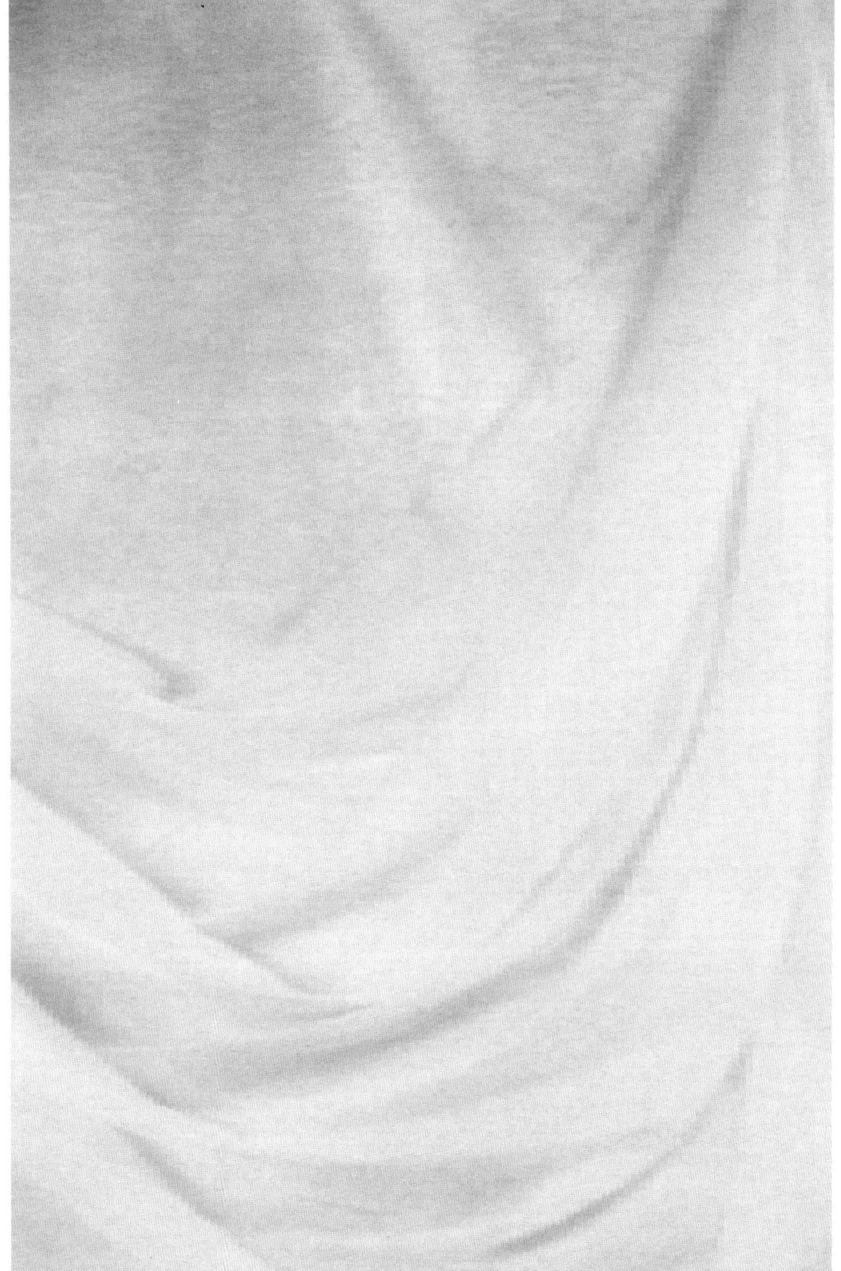

Did You Know?

Women do ejaculate!
A woman's "love juice" is usually anywhere from ½ to 1 teaspoon of a milky, non-staining substance.

Naughty Game

#14

Harem Nights

Create an oasis in your home!

Harem Nights

Men who show a little creativity and imagination will quickly win the heart of the woman they love. You don't even need to leave the house to create an aura of mystery and seduction that will have her smiling secretly for days to come. One common desire for women is that, despite all other competition, they are the chosen one! Tonight you will make your lover know that she is the most magnificent, desirable creature on earth in Harem Nights.

Begin by transforming your bedroom into an exotic, erotic wonderland with a Middle Eastern feel. Hang a white sheet from the ceiling, over your bed, draped around all four corners. Assemble throw pillows to provide a comfortable, plush arena for play. Scatter candles of varying shapes and sizes throughout the room, and prepare incense burners to heighten the atmosphere. Leave a plate of figs and grapes on the bedside table to tantalize her taste buds in preparation for the night's game of acquisition and conquering climax.

When you are ready to begin, take your woman by the hand and let her know you have chosen her, above all others, to be your concubine. Admire her attributes - her flowing hair, full lips, and soft curves. Touch and caress each part of her body with reverence and admiration. Then, take her by the hand and lead her to your chamber of love.

After you settle her gently among all the pillows on the bed, light the candles and incense, and return to sit by her side. Pamper her with your attentions. Speak softly, lovingly, and with devotion. Feed her with your fingers first, then playfully place a piece of fruit between your teeth and allow her to share and suck this symbol of desire from your lips to her own. Undress her slowly, fondling her breasts, running your fingers across her belly, then slipping them into her wet fountain of desire. Take her and make her yours.

As you rest, fully sated, she will know that she will always be the only one for you, with memories forever of Harem Nights.

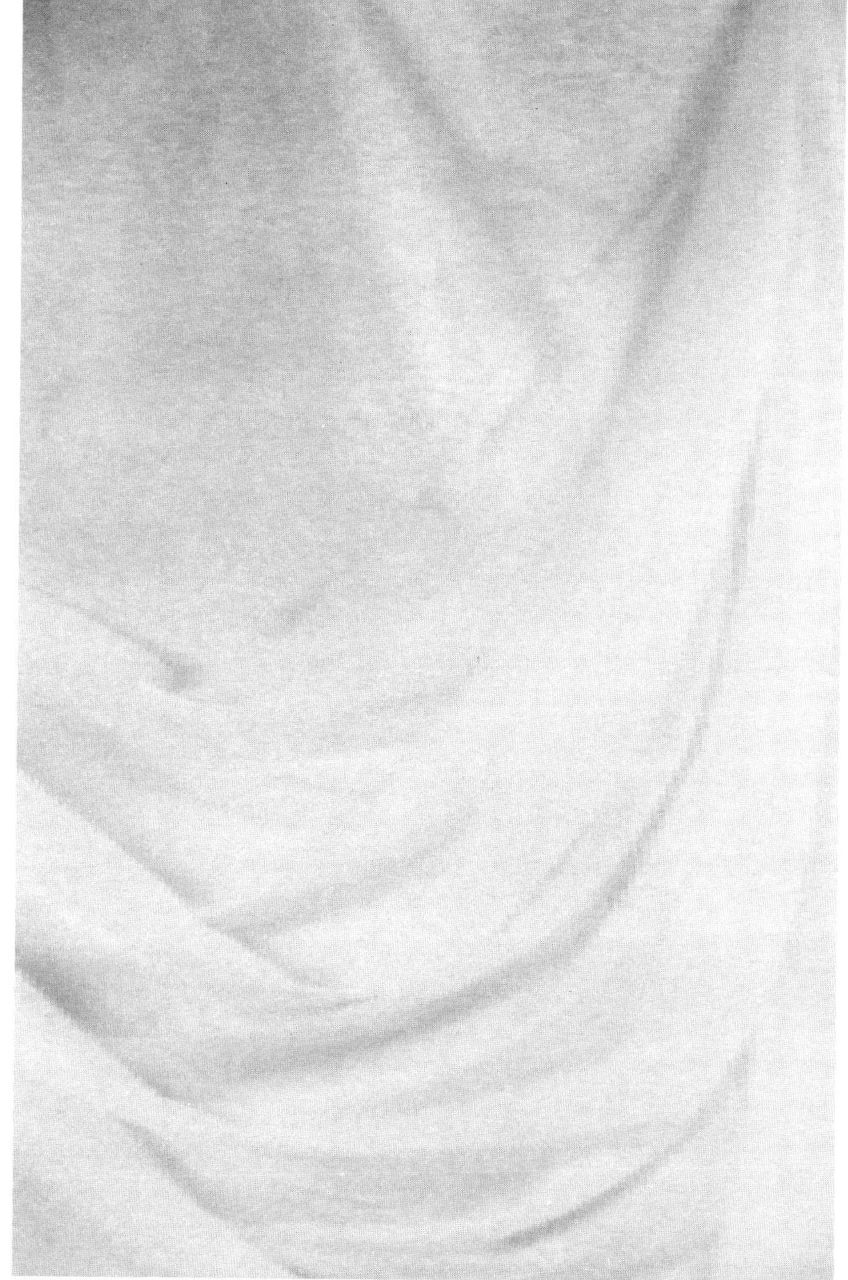

Keeping It Up

Young men "raise the flag" automatically.
With time and the security of a long-term
relationship, men need three things to
become sexually aroused:
Intimacy
Pleasure
Eroticism

Naughty Game

#15

Fun With Figures

Your mission,
should you decide to accept it...

Fun with Figures

How is your basic arithmetic? Just as surely as you know that 2+2=4, you also know that your man is excited about figures of another kind - the female kind! This is not a time to become jealous or insecure. The best thing you can do for yourself, your man, and your relationship is to accept it, embrace it, and even encourage it! Today's game may seem like *Mission Impossible*, but with a little confidence in yourself, you'll soon discover Fun with Figures!

Your Mission, if you decide to accept it, is to surround your lover with images of the female form. Using magazine centerfolds, posters, and photos of yourself, you are going to temporarily wallpaper the walls of a small bathroom in your home. Create a collage of naked female beauty on every inch of the room, including the ceiling, if possible.

When you have finished preparing the room, be sure to close the door to ensure the element of surprise. Concoct some excuse to lure him into this newly decorated brothel filled with "figures" and fun! Once inside, close the door and enjoy his sheer amazement as he admires your efforts. Start to strip your own clothes away, proud to be the one living, breathing example amidst the sensuous surroundings.

Your healthy, hot-blooded man is becoming aroused by now. You are going to take charge and bring him to a full and overwhelming climax of sensational sex. Fully naked, start to urgently rip away his clothes. Let him know you are as aroused as he is. Urge him to look and admire the pictures as well as you. This is not the time to be coy or gentle. Passion is for the moment and the moment is NOW!

After you have him fully undressed, start to stroke his sword firmly, masterfully, with one purpose in mind: his surging sexual release. Talk to him. Point out the tits in one picture, the shaved pussy in another. Forget yourself for the moment and concentrate on his pure lust. Because it is your body he is touching and loving, your body that will lie down with him tonight, after his Fun with Figures!

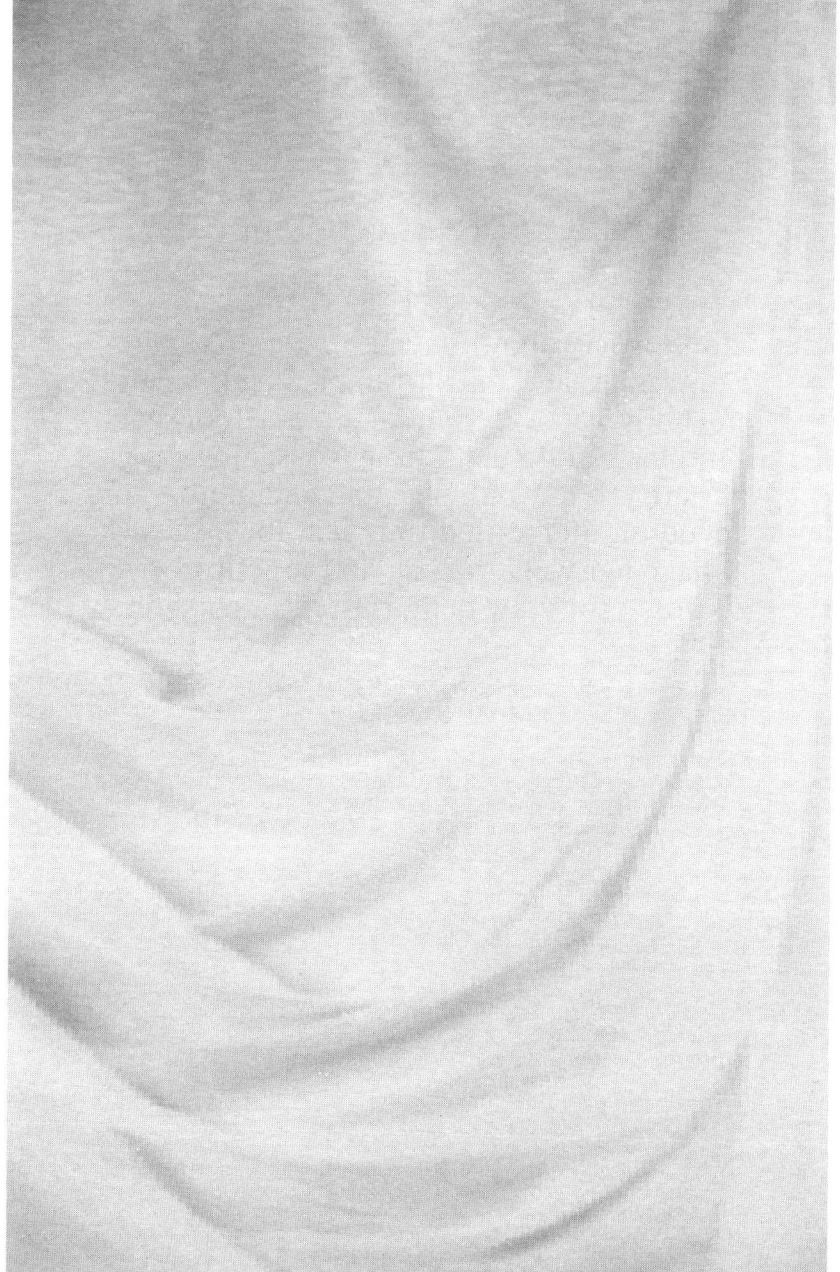

Looking for Her Secret Spots?

Her secret spot is NOT the G-spot! Men, don't worry about having to identify any one given area! Concentrate, instead, on <u>any</u> one body part – her shoulder, her foot, her temples – and spend time massaging just that area. Your patience and willingness to spend uninterrupted time just for her will have her wet, craving, and practically weeping for your penetrating conclusion!

Naughty Game

#16

My Tutor

You'll be the teacher's pet!

My Tutor

Despite years of being together, many couples find that they still don't know everything they should about what arouses the other. Tonight's game will help overcome that obstacle as you ask your lady to be your Tutor - for a fee!

Preparation for this game is simple. Collect 20 one-dollar bills and present them to your lover. Tell her that you want to learn more about the things that excite her, the acts that make her wet, and the foreplay that she fantasizes about. Instruct her to pay you with a one dollar bill every time you touch, kiss or probe her in a way that feels good. While this may feel risky because you are opening yourself up to admitting that you don't know her as well as you could, the rewards will be countless.

Darken the bedroom, as this is usually more comfortable for a woman. Avoid adding music, liquor or incense to the atmosphere, as you want an honest response to your actions. Start with something you know from the past is a sure winner - kiss her neck, nibble on her breasts, or stoke the inside of her thigh. Listen for an increased rhythm in her breathing or an audible sigh. And, of course, wait for her to slip you the first of 20 one-dollar bills.

Continue to experiment with different touches and different parts of her body. Have you ever tried sucking on her big toe? Perhaps you should experiment with slipping a finger into her anus. Are you always gentle when fondling her tits? Maybe she will be even more aroused if you tweak her nipples with a firmer command! Give her a slap on the buttocks and see if you win a prize. Take a risk, because you are asking her to do the same in honestly sharing with you her feelings of arousal.

For those who remain a little shy about saying what feels good, allowing your lover to Tutor you with the non-verbal payment of a one-dollar bill can teach you more in one night than you've known all these many years! Enjoy!

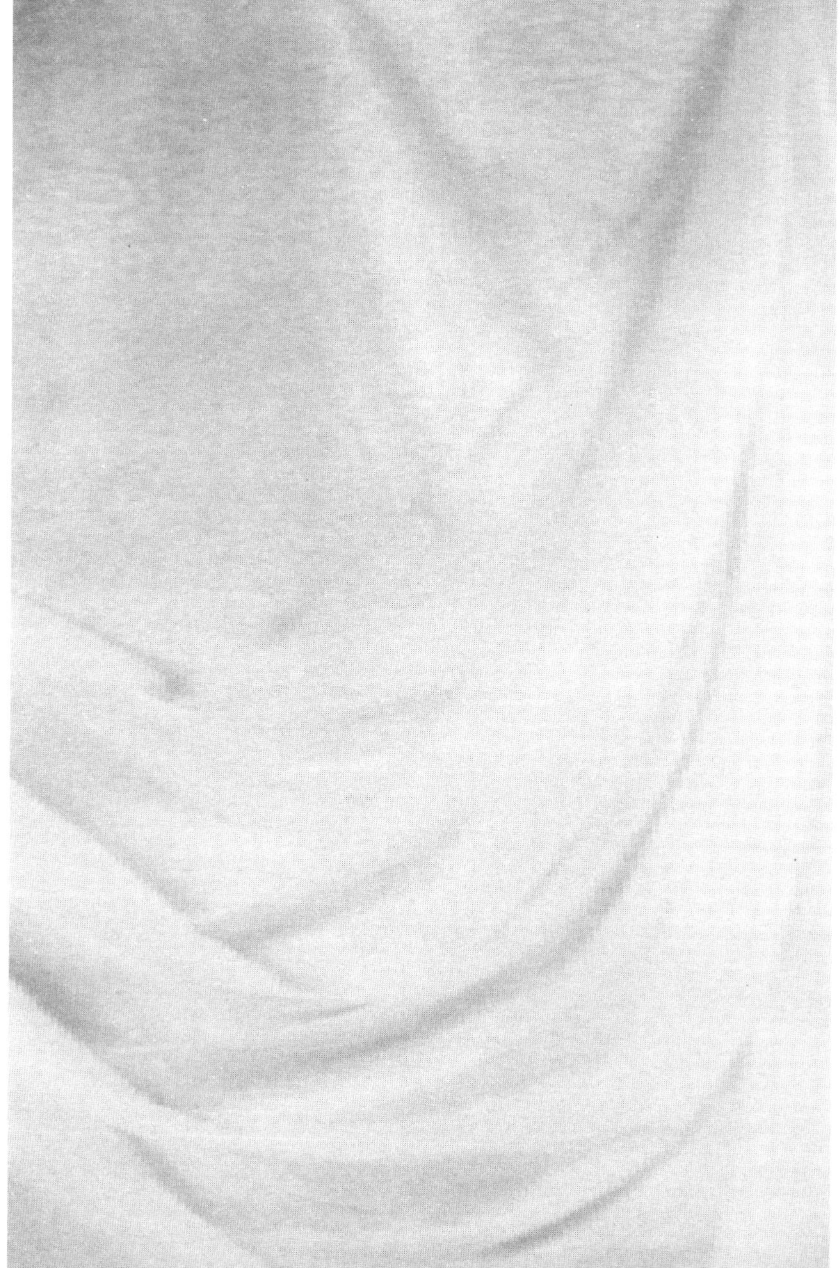

Looking for His Secret Spots?

Try these:

Buttocks
Balls
Ears
Nipples
Perineum
Inner Thigh
Anus

Naughty Game

#17

Lady Of The Night

She's not selling girl scout cookies!

Lady Of The Night

To rekindle and fuel your passion for each other, it is often wise to walk on the wild side, surprising your lover with one of his fantasies. While many men have never indulged their dream of being with a Lady Of The Night, you are going to ensure that you are the one who will ring his bell.

Every man craves a woman who can exhibit good breeding one moment, and be a wild and wicked whore in bed the next. This is a game you can really have fun with. When you assume the role of Lady Of The Night, you will light his fire, while at the same time live out some of your own secret desires, turning yourself from a lady into a tramp.

Assemble your outfit with care. Consider color first. Red is the color historically associated with sex, fiery and sassy at the same time. Purple would be another good choice, as it symbolizes passion. Style is important - it must be tight, brief, and suggestive. A Merry Widow, with garters and stockings, covered by a tiny skirt sends a clear message. Short shorts, over knee boots and a see-through blouse, says it all too. Be creative. Accessorize with lots of gold chains and wrist bangles, add a mole to your cheek or a temporary tattoo to your breast. Go heavy with your make-up, using fire engine red for your lips and cheeks. Add a wig for extra drama.

While your man is relaxing after dinner, watching TV or reading the paper, tell him you're heading off to take a long, soaking bubble bath. Run the water, and turn on a radio in the bathroom to create the illusion that you are happily occupied. After you dress for the game, slip out a back door and make your way to the front. Prop one hand against the wall, the other on your hip as you ring the bell.

When he opens the door, in a low, sultry voice tell him, "I understand you're looking for some fun. Gabriella sent me," as you push your way past him and close the door behind you. "I am your Lady Of The Night - let's get down to business!"

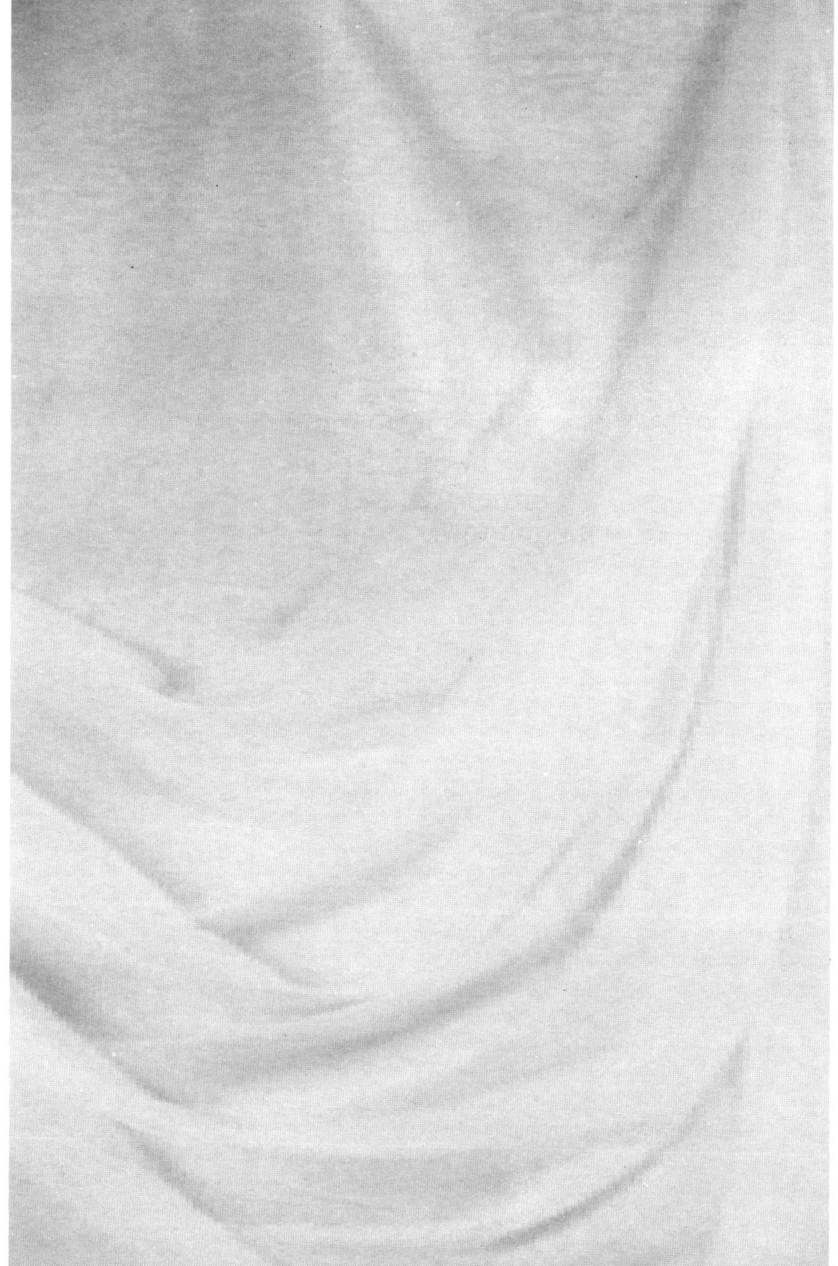

Excuses Women Use Why Not To Have Sex

"I have a headache..."
"My hair is dirty..."
"The draperies aren't hanging right..."
"My mother might call..."
"Dinner will burn..."
"The neighbors will hear..."
"My legs are hairy..."
"The batteries in the vibrator are dead..."
"You've had a long day..."
"My leather corset is at the dry cleaners..."

Naughty Game

#18

Super Cybersex

Take your lust online!

Super Cybersex

In this day and age, using the Internet to send messages of all kinds is as easy and trustworthy as the old Pony Express. Most people have access to E-mail either at home or at work, or both. You are going to use this medium to send some hot, steamy suggestions to your sweetheart about tonight's activities in this game of Super Cybersex!!

It's best if you can E-mail her at work, because the naughtiness of the message will have more of an impact on her when she is in her professional surroundings. Add to that the necessity of waiting to consummate your suggestions, and you will have her wiggling in her seat all day, and wet and willing by the time she arrives home.

While you may want to create your own message, or personalize it in some way, here is a tried and true beginning to your own erotic E-mail:

"Star Sirius - brightest and most perfect in my universe. I am sitting here flooded with images of you - your silky hair, your haunting eyes and those luscious lips which turn up ever so slightly when I walk into the room. Part them for me, baby, and imagine my tongue flicking across your lips and disappearing deep within your warm mouth. Feel my fingertips caressing your cheeks, trailing down your neck and around to your back where I can unhook your bra, releasing your soft tits. They are hungry for my touch. They show me your need as your nipples harden quickly beneath the gentle kneading of my fingers, followed by the lapping of my tongue and the gentle pressure of my teeth upon your flesh. Now picture this: someone is watching, hidden in the shadows, his own excitement heightened by the soft moans escaping your mouth. His tension is palpable as I reach up under your skirt and ease aside your panties as my forefinger finds its way into your dripping cunt, followed by a second finger, then a third. My thumb brushes against your clit as you become a heaving vision of the perfect orgasm. Come for me, baby. Come home. I'll be waiting..."

Excuses Men Use Why Not to Have Sex

Naughty Game

#19

Afternoon Delight

As the sun is setting,
He will be rising...

Afternoon Delight

In today's world of more conveniences, but less time; more knowledge, but less wisdom; more rushing about, but less accomplished; more forms of communication, but less real understanding; more money and possessions, but less love - it's time to step back, relax and plan a little Afternoon Delight!

It takes so little effort to make special memories with the one you love. But it does take a little ingenuity to break away from the routines and the drudgery of everyday life. This game is designed to be initiated quickly, with virtually no advance planning. When your lives are feeling just a bit too hectic, and you really feel you have no time to spare, remember how valuable an hour or two can be in restoring your passion as well as your energy and sanity.

Late in the afternoon, when the sun is beginning to set, suggest to your lover that you take a quick trip to the park or beach - someplace outdoors yet peaceful. Take along a couple of blankets - one to spread on the ground, and one to cover yourselves with.

Settle down side by side and take a few deep breaths of the fresh air. Remember that you are here to please your man, so limit conversation and begin stroking him. Let your fingertips drift across his forehead and down his cheek, outlining his lips. Lean forward to kiss him and nibble his ear as your hands slither under the blanket for regions below. Over the fabric of his pants, massage his cock until you feel it growing hard beneath your touch. Unbutton and unzip his slacks, easing his throbbing member from its confines. Use your body (and the blanket over you) to conceal your activities. Stroke him with full thrusts of your hand. Take a moment to moisten your hand with saliva, then go back to work. Vary the rhythm of your strokes until he nears explosion, then make them firm and fast until he can no longer contain himself, coming in the aftermath of a simple Afternoon Delight.

Imagination!

A little experimentation, combined with imagination, results in getting rid of the boredom of your normal routines! What could YOU do with some of the everyday items you have around the house?

A roll of electrical tape
A hairbrush
A lambswool duster
A bottle of olive oil
A frond from your fern plant
A cotton swab

Naughty Game

#20

Her Best Friend

And you thought
three was a crowd!

Her Best Friend

Every woman has at least one Best Friend, but tonight you are going to help her meet another. For if you are ever unable to be with her and satisfy her, you'll want to know that she has a very Best Friend to take care of her cravings - a Best Friend you can always trust!

No, her new Best Friend is not another woman, and certainly not another man! Her Best Friend is a replication of your long and hard cock - a dildo! Dildos come in many shapes and sizes. Some have ridges, many vibrate, but all can be adequate substitutes when the main man isn't around!

Even if you already own a dildo, go out and buy another one. Be more daring the second time around. Try something different and a little wild. Remember, while it is a substitute for you, it can never replace the real thing!

When you are ready to enact this game, spend a little time preparing your lover for the evening's adventure. Tease her a little. Tell her you want to introduce her to something that will double your pleasure together. With her curiosity piqued, shush her and tell her to wait for the introductions.

Hide the dildo nearby, perhaps in your bedside table. Spend some time on foreplay (which you already initiated when you talked to her about a mysterious addition to your lovemaking.) Undress her lovingly. Lead her to your bed. Smother her with kisses. Spread oil upon her body and massage it firmly into her thirsty skin. When she begins moaning for more, reach for the dildo and begin to use it as a tool for pleasure. Let it vibrate upon her hardening nipples. Run it along her tummy and down her thighs. Titillate her by running it over your own body as well. Move it slowly and methodically between her legs, over her clit, then away again. Her breathing will be heavy as you taunt and tease her new Best Friend around the fringes of her excitement. Ease it gently into her waiting pussy, probing as if with your own hardened cock. She'll love her new Best Friend - and you!

Attitude is Everything

The sexiest women are <u>not</u> the ones with the perkiest tits, the taut butt, the tiny waist, or the long, slender legs. The sexiest women are the ones who <u>think</u> they are sexy!

Naughty Game

#21

Viva La Difference!

Maid to please!

Viva La Difference!

Ready to get a little frisky and free? Forget that you have been striving for equal rights and equal pay. In this sexcapade, you are going to realize that sometimes the old methods are, in fact, the tried and true ones! You are going to assume the role of French Maid for your lover and in doing so, you'll be ready to shout, "Viva La Difference!"

If you don't own an apron, go buy one - preferably a sheer and lacy concoction. Dust off a silver tray. Invest in a fine bottle of brandy, fill two snifters and place them on the tray with some hors d'oeuvres. When your man arrives home from work, greet him at the door wearing only the apron and high heels, the tray held invitingly above your head, uplifting your naked breasts. Lower your eyes with a small curtsey, and welcome home the master of the house.

Usher him into the living room, then offer him a drink. As you place the tray upon the coffee table, be sure to bend gracefully for him to admire the view from behind. If he playfully reaches to caress your assets, step aside with a demure smile, a little laugh, and tell him, "No, no Monsieur!"

Kneel at his feet; remove his shoes and socks. Making and maintaining eye contact, massage his toes, his arches, reaching up under his pant legs to stimulate the muscles in his tight lower calves. As you do, you'll be stimulating many a muscle in his entire body - especially the one you are most seeking! Slowly, serve him by removing his clothes.

Take advantage of your power and rise to offer him another brandy or a morsel of food. Cross the room to turn on some mood music. You'll be turning on far more than sounds to fill the air. Let him admire and desire your flesh. Untie the apron and let it drop to the floor. Smile and tell him, "I'm here to take care of ALL your needs, Monsieur!"

Many a woman has feared that such servitude was demeaning. It's not! Kick off your shoes and kick up your heels as you experience first-hand the power it actually bestows you as you experience, "Viva La Difference!"

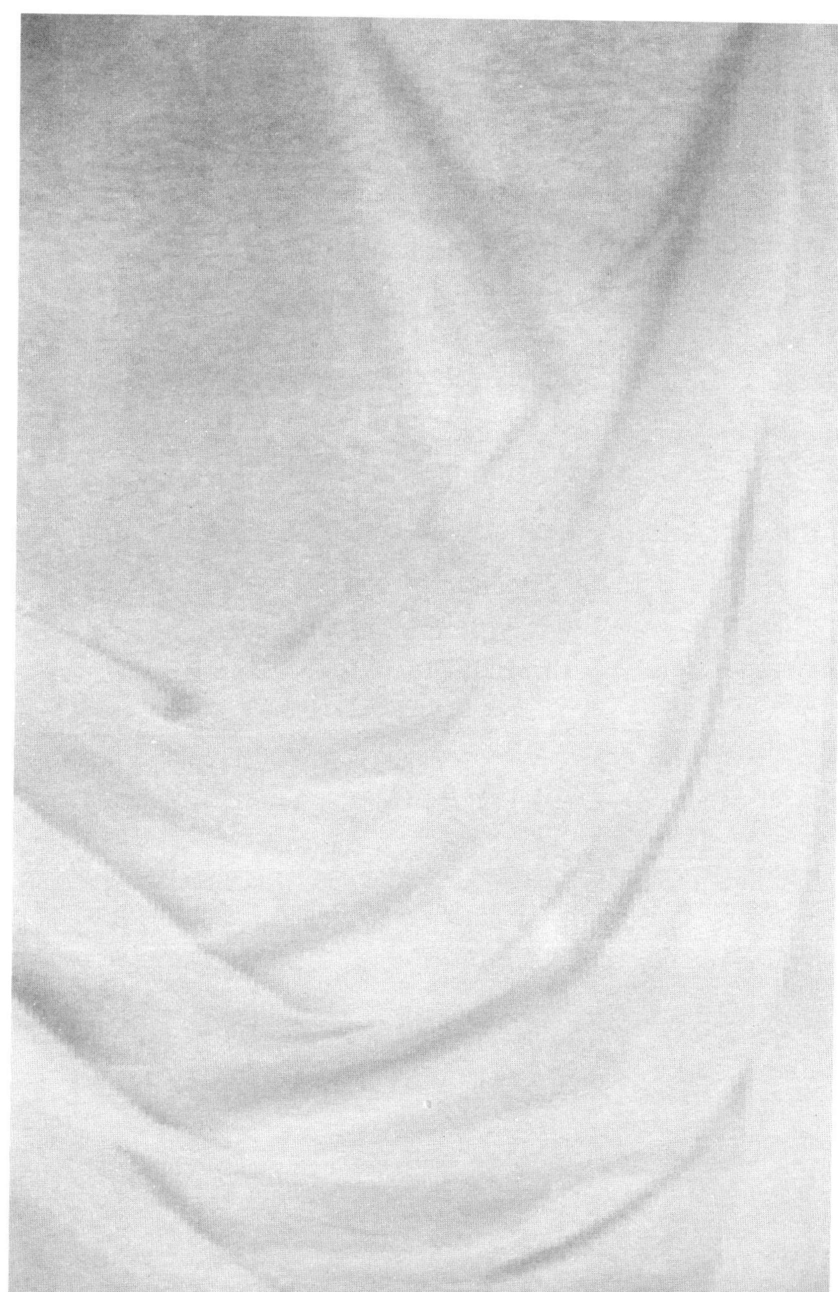

Acting Out Fantasies
(For Him)

Cowboy
Priest
Gigolo
Delivery Boy
Movie Director
Slave
Gynecologist
Police Man
Construction Worker

Naughty Game

#22

The Sexual Trivia Test

Excuse me,
do I know you?

The Sexual Trivia Test

Even couples who have been together for a long time are bound to find that there is a lot they still don't know about one another's sexual experiences, dreams and fantasies. Take the following Sexual Trivia Test - twice - first answering the questions about yourself, and then guessing the answers of your lover. Have your sweetheart do the same. Tonight, compare notes with her and whoever answers the most questions correctly about the other wins. "And what is the prize?" you ask. See the last question!

1. Who was the first naked person I touched?
2. My favorite body part on me? You?
3. My least favorite body part on me? You?
4. My favorite excuse not to make love is...?
5. What comes to mind when I think "hot and spicy"?
6. My favorite fantasy is...
7. I've had sex with _____ people.
8. I lost my virginity at age...
9. How many orgasms have I ever had at one time?
10. I confide most/all our secrets to ______________.
11. The one thing I would change about me is...
12. The one thing I would change about you is...
13. Last time we made love, it was a _____on a scale of 1-10.
14. My most embarrassing sexual experience was...
15. My favorite sexual position is...
16. I wish you would spend more time doing...
17. One thing we've never tried, but I'd like to is...
18. Would I make love to a stranger for $1,000,000?
19. Would I let you make love to a stranger for $1,000,000?
20. The most unusual place I've ever made love was...
21. I masturbate ______ (how often)?
22. The quality I like most about myself is...
23. If I "win" I want you to...

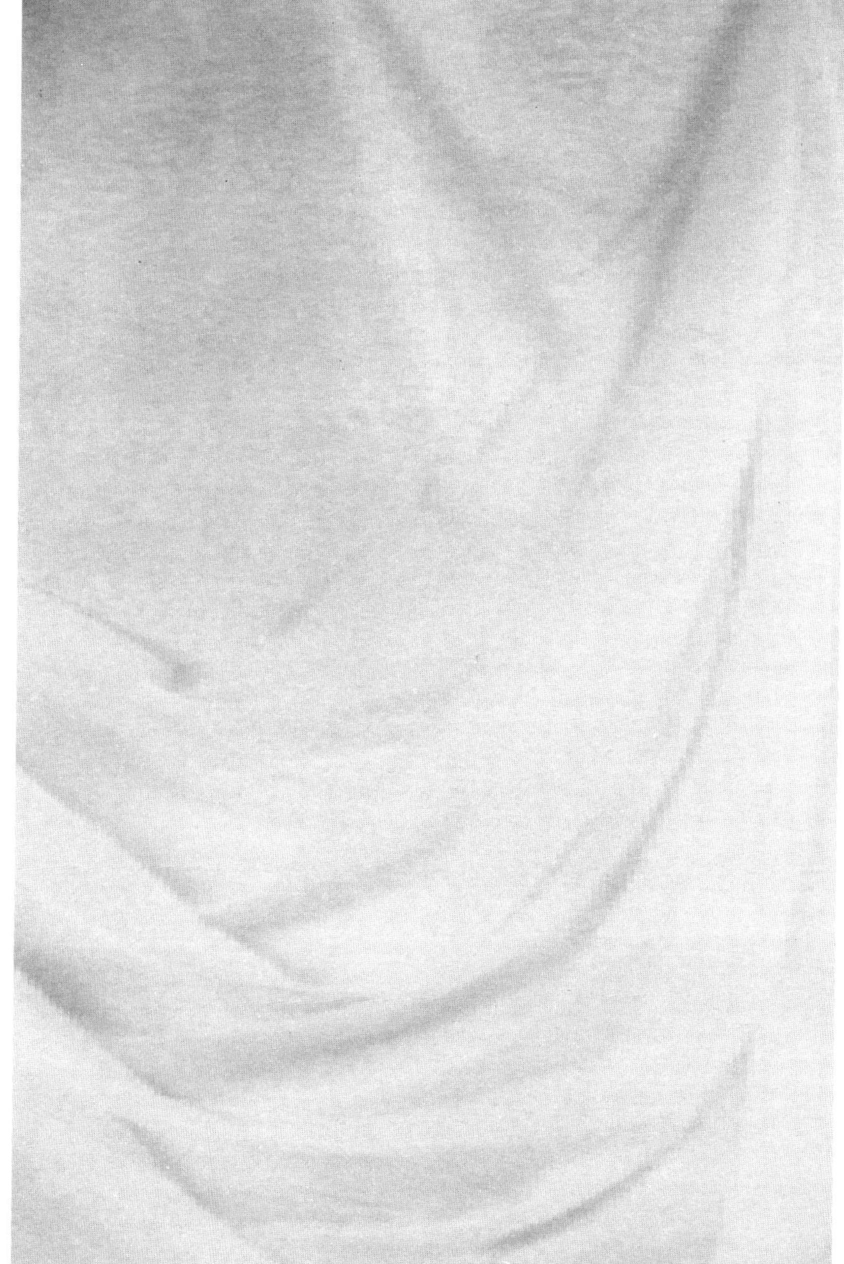

Acting Out Fantasies
(For Her)

Virgin
Librarian
Cheerleader
Stewardess
Prostitute
Farmer's Daughter
Sex Therapist
Teacher

Naughty Game

#23

Spin the Bottle

A very "adult" version of a children's game

Spin the Bottle

Remember the days when an innocent game of Spin the Bottle set your juices running? Well, you're a big girl now, and while the name of the game remains the same, the rules are so very different!

This is a very easy game to initiate. All it takes is a sense of adventure on your part, and a willingness to take your sex life to new heights with a few simple props. Instead of playing Spin the Bottle with a group of nervous, giggly pre-teens, this adult version is a game just for two.

Clear a section of your living room floor and create a circle of the following props: a peeled carrot, a cigar, a long zucchini, a banana, a tube of toothpaste, and a fat sausage. Use your imagination to look around your house. As you probably can tell, you are creating an array of items that your lover will use on you in a foreplay extravaganza. The last item you will need is a glass bottle. Select a nice bottle of chilled wine, placing it upright in the center of the circle. After you have enjoyed its contents, the game will begin.

When your lover arrives home from work, he will undoubtedly be curious about the new arrangement in your living room. Let him wonder as he changes into something more comfortable. Present him with a corkscrew and two wine goblets, and ask him to pour a toast to a night of ecstasy. When the bottle has been emptied, place it in the center of the circle and give it a spin. Then lay down on the couch or the floor, spread your legs invitingly, and let him know you are ready for him to give you pleasure. Guide him to gently probe your pussy with the chosen prop. Use a water-soluble jelly as needed for lubrication. Run your hands over your own body as you feel the friction of a new sword piercing your pulsing hole. Allow yourself a few minutes to savor the new sensation, then ask him to Spin the Bottle again. Keep playing the game until the only prop you want is the one bulging in his pants, ready to finish you off with screams of delight.

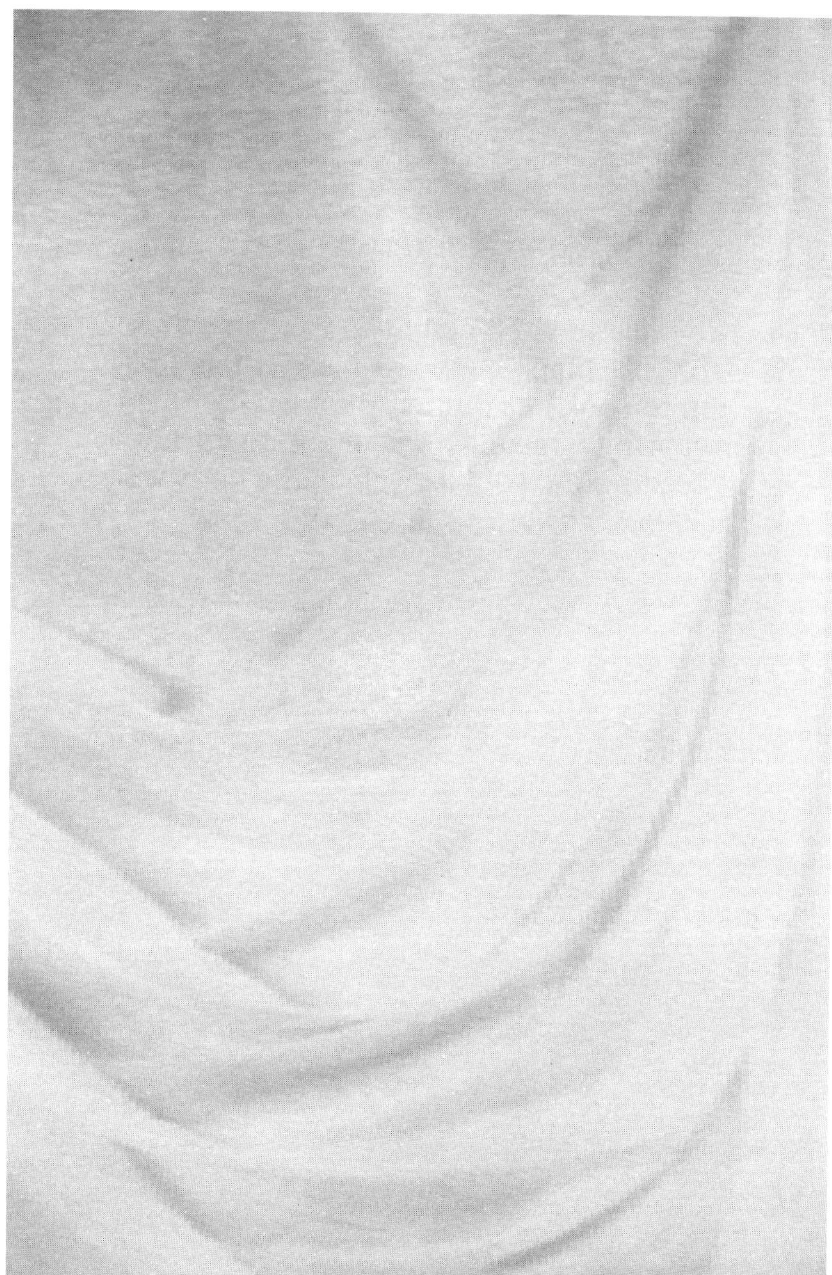

What Women Want

The most desired activity a woman wants from the man she is involved with is for him to cook her dinner. Women identify preparing a meal with signs of nurturing, feeding the soul as well as the body.

Naughty Game

#24

In the Mood

You'll have her where you want her!

In the Mood

Smart men know that a woman is not always, or as easily, In the Mood for love as their male counterparts, especially after several years together with the same lover and the same routines. Men may be perfectly happy with having sex the same way, at the same time, in the same place. Women, however, seem to crave the occasional flight of fantasy, the unexpected. You are going to prove yourself to be a very smart man when you take this opportunity to get her In the Mood.

An average man will know to send his lover a gift at work for special occasions, such as her birthday, their anniversary, or Valentine's Day. This lets her co-workers know that she is loved and makes her feel special. But the smart man knows to send his lover an unexpected gift for seemingly no reason at all. That kind of gesture really raises her to new levels in the eyes of the people she works with. In turn, you will win her undying devotion and get very lucky, because you will get her In the Mood.

Visit a sexy lingerie shop found easily in virtually every mall in the country. Buy her a matching g-string or thong and a set of pasties. Then find a card shop or grocery store that carries helium balloons. Ask them to insert your gifts into the balloon before filling it with air. Have the balloon delivered to her place of work, with a notecard instructing her to wear her gifts when she gets home. (You may want to advise her to pop the balloon in private if a public display of your lust could lead to embarrassment!)

When she arrives home, have one more surprise waiting for her - YOU - in a matching thong of your own! Strip away her outer garments to unearth the sexy image you have been carrying in your mind all day. Take her right then and there, on the floor just feet away from your front door. Tug off her pasties, then cover her tits with kisses to soothe and arouse. For a smart lover, such as you, every woman is In the Mood!

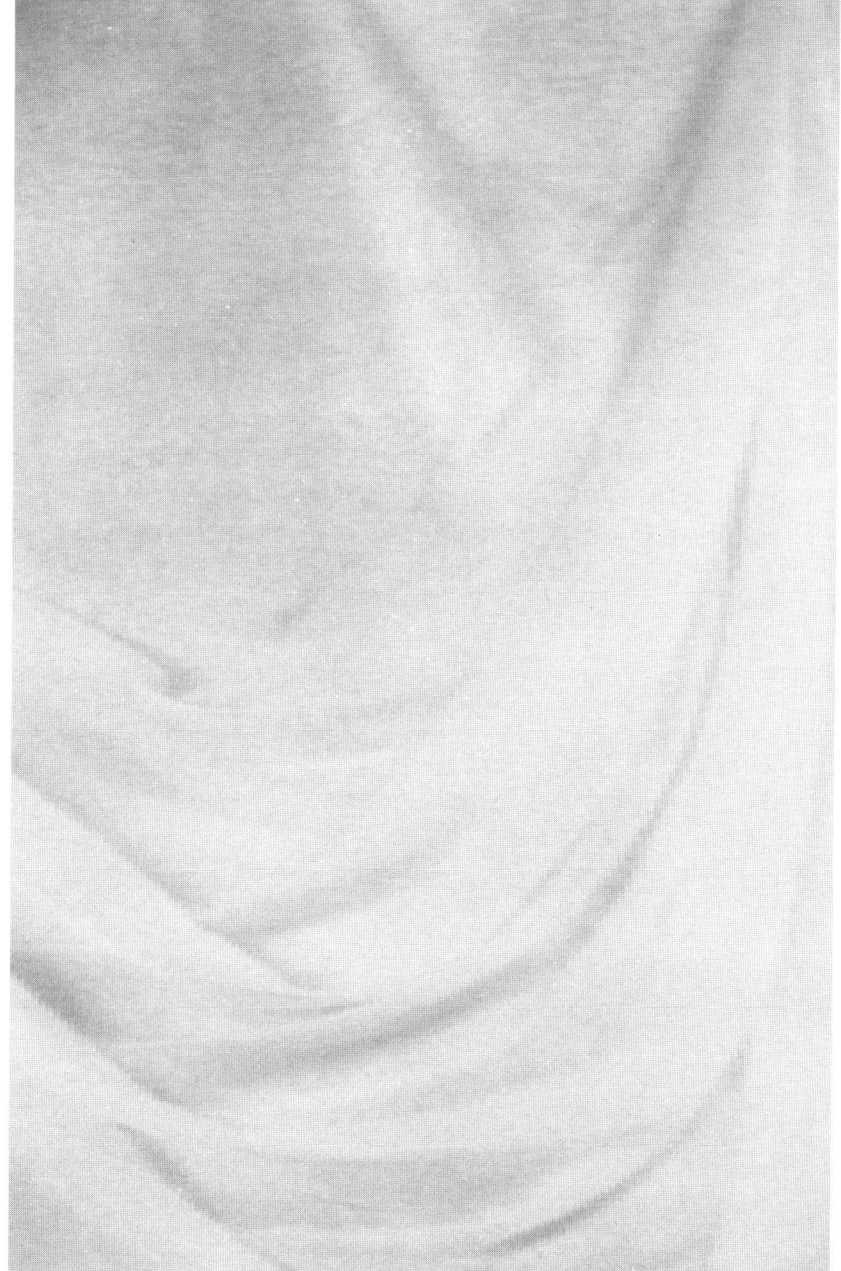

Pet Peeve

Ladies, does it hurt your feelings that your man is sound asleep almost immediately after making love with you? Know this: even without the physical exertion and release that comes from sex, the average person falls asleep in just seven minutes! So as he is drifting off to sweet dreams, know that your love-making simply accelerated the process.

Naughty Game
#25

Dinner At The Ritz

Guess who's coming
AT dinner!

Dinner at the Ritz

When you think of a five star restaurant, you think of candlelight, soft music, and a five course meal: soup, salad, sherbet to cleanse the palette, the main entrée, and a decadent dessert. After you serve your own Dinner at the Ritz, no other restaurant will ever hold a candle to tonight's soiree. Your courses will be of a very different nature, far more satisfying than the most prize-winning delicacies offered in the most famous bistros the world around.

To serve up your "specialties", you must create the proper ambiance with scattered candles, flowers, and romantic music. Set a table with your best linens. Using posterboard, prepare the following menu of tonight's delights, then place it in clear view on the table. Dress elegantly, and when he arrives home from work, be ready to act as hostess to serve the first course, then second.... His own "hard cookie" will be ready to be devoured by the third, then stuffed inside your "moist shortbread" by the final course! BON APPETIT!

First Course

Sweetly seasoned kisses on the eyes, tip of nose, and earlobe, with slightly salty probing of tongue

Second Course

With all outer coverings removed, warm oil spread evenly across breast of man

Third Course

(Cleanse the Palette)

Frothy frozen yogurt swirled first in the mouth, followed by a deep throat encasement of the penis muscle

Fourth Course

A fully stripped breast and leg of woman meant to be eaten heartily

Final Course

A triple layered mixture of a long, hard cookie stuffed inside a warm, moist shortbread, filled with cream

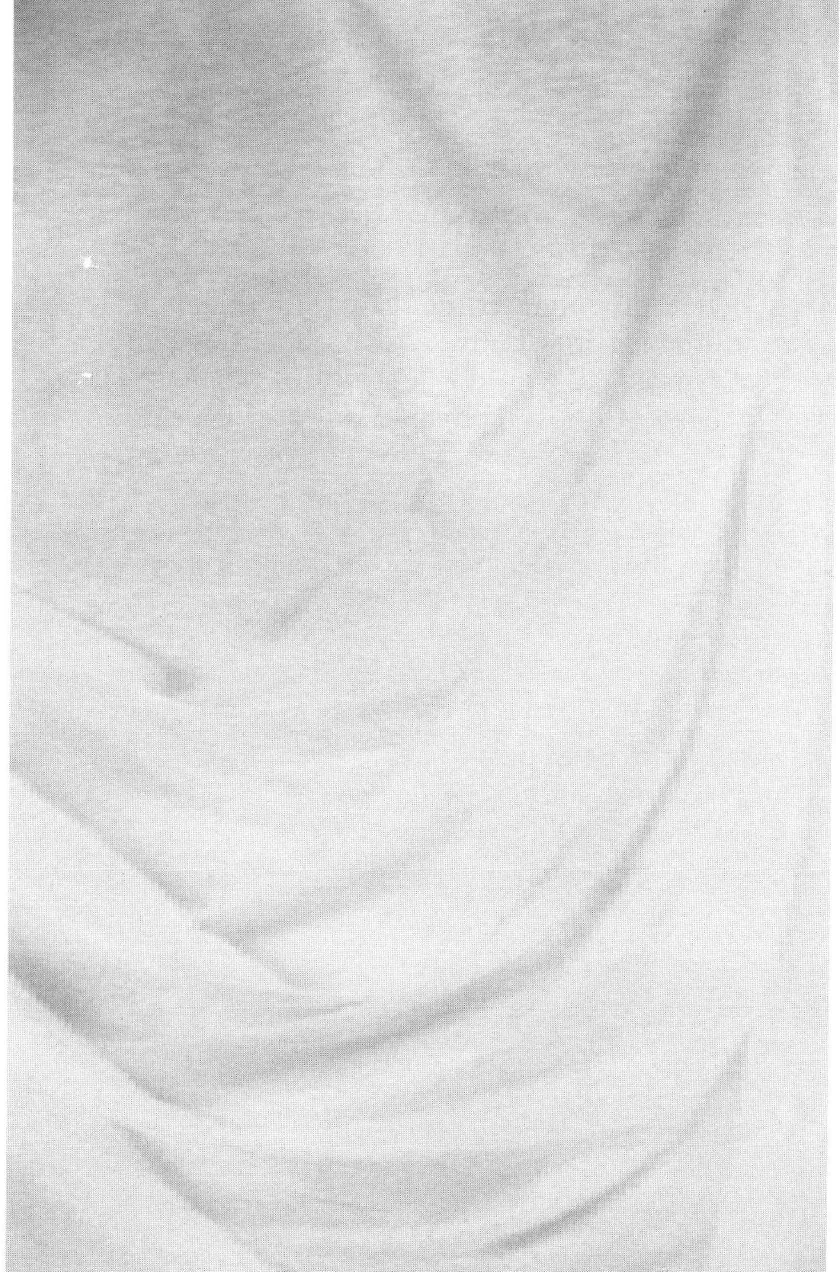

Fight or Flight

When confronted with conflict, there is a basic, animal instinct known as the "Fight or Flight Syndrome." We either gear up for battle or run away. Choose your battles carefully and consider an alternative –
FLOW!

Naughty Game
#26

Camping Under The Sheets

You'll earn your merit badge tonight!

Camping Under the Sheets

You're a man! You love the great outdoors! It brings out the animal in you, the wild side that wants to get down and dirty! How can you bring the great outdoors inside? Just go Camping Under the Sheets!

Camping brings us back to the plain and simple pleasures in life. Sex is one of those plain and simple pleasures! It doesn't have to be complicated or fancy; it doesn't have to cost an arm and a leg; and it doesn't have to involve extravagant planning, time or money. But great sex, after you've been together for awhile, does involve a little ingenuity. Break the routine, the mold. Try something different! Forget the five-minute missionary position and treat your lover to an adventure. All you need is your bed and a flashlight.

After the two of you have gone to bed for the night, pull the sheets high up over your heads, turn on a flashlight, illuminating her face. Be playful; shine the light all around underneath the sheets and suggest you get cozy by stripping off each other's clothes. Help her wiggle out of her garments all the while keeping the sheet covering you both. Then go exploring. Tell her you need to find some hard little nuggets to nourish you, then pounce on her nipples until they arise to the occasion. Show her the larger nuts, hard and tasty between your legs. Take her hand and guide it to your hardened cock, letting her know she has found the firewood to ignite the fires needed for the night. Take your flashlight, be the good Boy Scout, and go looking for the bushes - her bush, that is - where you can build your fire of intense heat and desire. Plunge your firestick into her bush and fuel those flames until they are doused with an explosion of white, frothy come - your own version of a fire extinguisher. It's always good to be prepared, and you both will always know you have what it takes to build the fires...and then put them out...when you go Camping Under the Sheets.

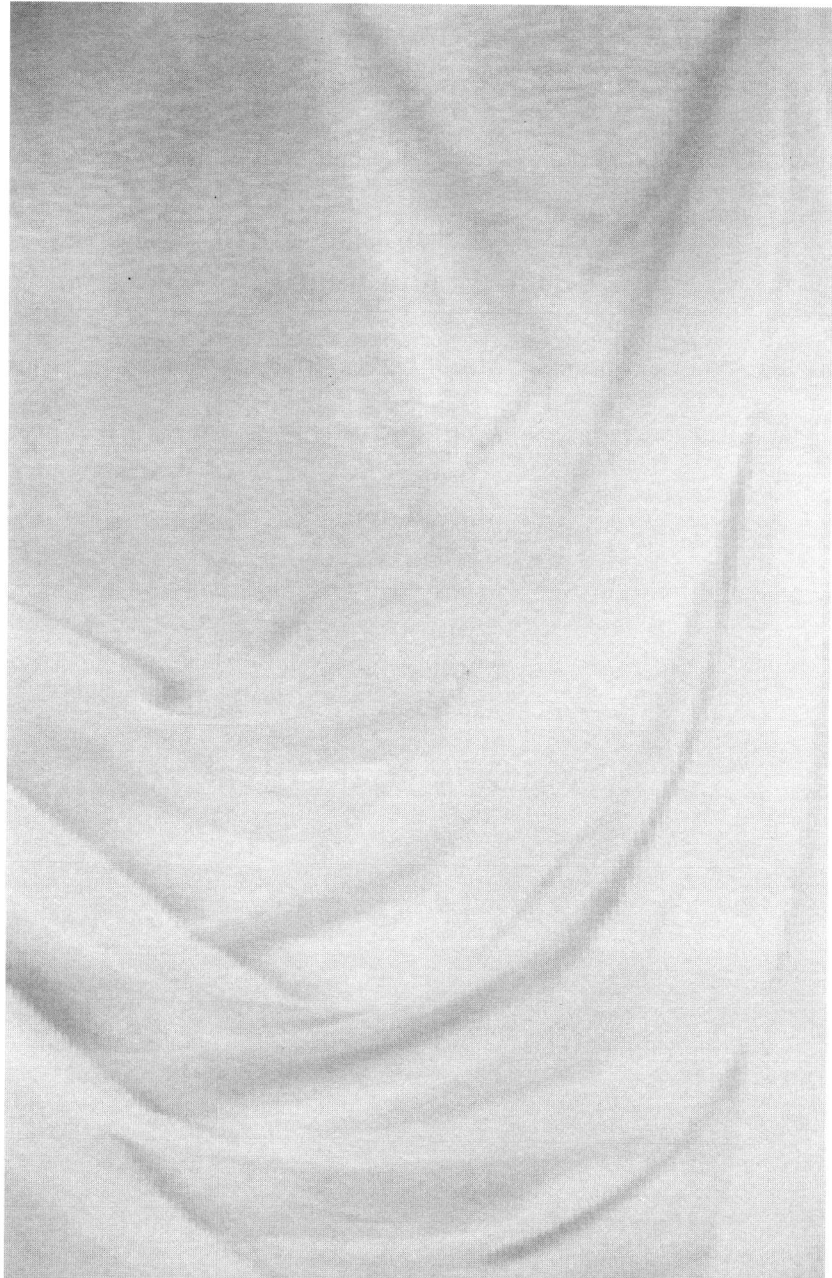

Five Vital Elements for a Happy Marriage

Make Love
Listen
Make Love
Apologize
Make Love
Forgive
Make Love
Support
Make Love
Touch

Did we mention MAKE LOVE?

Naughty Game

#27

Swing High,
Swing Low,
Swing Deep

Playground pleasures!

Swing High, Swing Low, Swing Deep

Recapturing some of the simple pleasures of your youth while adding a very adult twist is a sure way to spice up your sexual routine. Remember the feeling of exhilaration when you would go to the park and run to the swing set, ready to pump your way from a standstill to heights that took your breath away? That alone may not do it for you now, but with a little added incentive, you'll have your lover begging to go to the park, pumping not only his legs but also his iron rod into you as you Swing High, Swing Low, Swing Deep."

For this adventure, you'll want to wear a long, loose skirt - and nothing else underneath it! After the sun sets, and the veil of protective darkness covers the earth, you should find a nearby deserted park, ready to offer you a private playground for adult pleasures. Suggest an evening stroll after dinner. Watch the stars come out, feel the cool breeze on your faces. Be playful - instigate a little game of tag, roll in the grass, run to the swings and ask him to push you, slowly, gently at first, then higher. Jump from the swing and tell him it's his turn. As he takes his seat on the swing, instead of going behind him to push, face him and let him know that you have other ideas at the moment, your appetite, and other parts, wetted by the building excitement. Lean forward to kiss his lips, letting your tongue dance across his mouth, over and between his teeth, plunging deep inside to arouse his desires. Press your body close to his, as you ease your skirt just far enough up to allow you to straddle his lap. Lock your legs around his waist. Under the protective covering of your skirt, caress his cock, unzip his pants, and let it free as you guide it into your readied pussy. Tell him to push with his legs to start the swing in motion, and hang on for the ride of your life. As he pumps with his legs, your bodies swaying in motion to the rapidly increasing rhythm of the swing, you'll experience a whole new exhilaration - Swing High, Swing Low, Swing Deep.

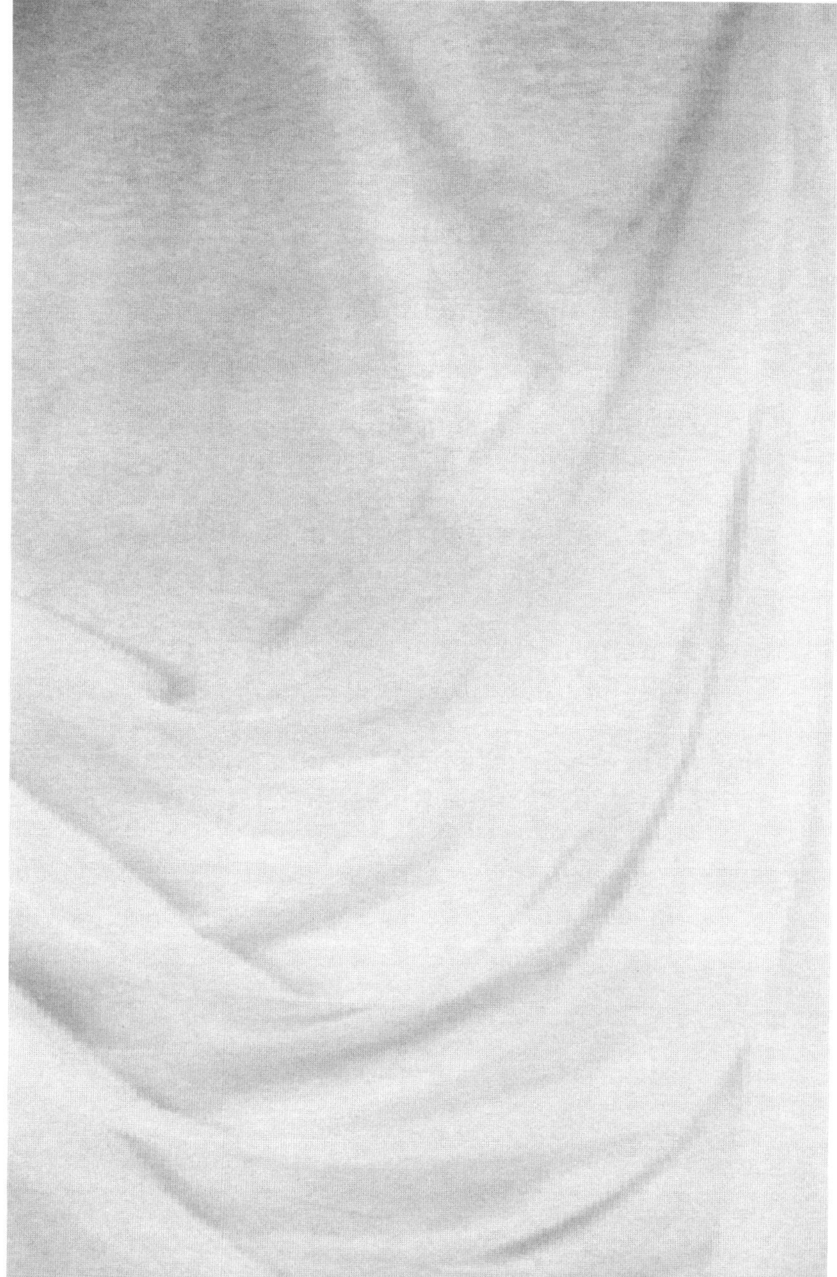

Understanding Women

To love a woman is to understand her...or at least pretend to.

For women, love is an occupation…smart men take on love as a second job.

Married women start appearing with green goop on their faces in the name of beauty.

Women are more creative than men…they need to tell men how great they are.

Diamonds are a girl's best friend and dogs are a man's - now who's smarter?

Naughty Game

#28

Mardi Gras

Man's search for
sexual pleasure

Mardi Gras

Each year hundreds of thousands of people converge on New Orleans to celebrate the ritualistic festival known as Mardi Gras. Characterized by a wild, hedonistic atmosphere, Mardi Gras symbolizes man's search for sexual pleasure. In your quest for new and daring ways to share passion with your lover, you are going to recreate a Mardi Gras adventure.

Mardi Gras involves crowds and, because of the distraction of so many people, sexual acts of all kinds go unnoticed - except by the willing participants. Sexual favors between strangers are exchanged for beads, so you must first purchase three or four strands of inexpensive bead necklaces to adorn your beloved. Next, choose a site for the enactment of your lust - like a crowded nightclub on a Saturday night.

As you dress for your evening out, present your lover with her gift of necklaces, simply saying that she must wear them for your pleasure. When you arrive at your chosen destination, tell her that within the hour you want to approach her as if you were a stranger. She must receive you, obey you, and be carried away by the spontaneity of the act. Order wine, dance together to the erotic, sensual beat of hot music among the hotter throng of thrill seekers. Arouse her, then send her away with the promise of returning.

Wait five or ten minutes. The sensation of being alone in the crowd will heighten her sensitivity. When you do approach her, lock eyes for a moment and then ask, "What will you give me for your beads?" Without waiting for her answer, slowly remove a strand of beads and tell her, "I want you to reach your hand down into my pants and grab hold of me - make me hot and hard." Position yourself so no one else can witness her submissive response. Press your body close to hers to shield you both from others, feel her tits pierce your chest, slip your hand underneath her shirt, pinching her hardened nipple, and let your passion COME in waves of decadent pleasure.

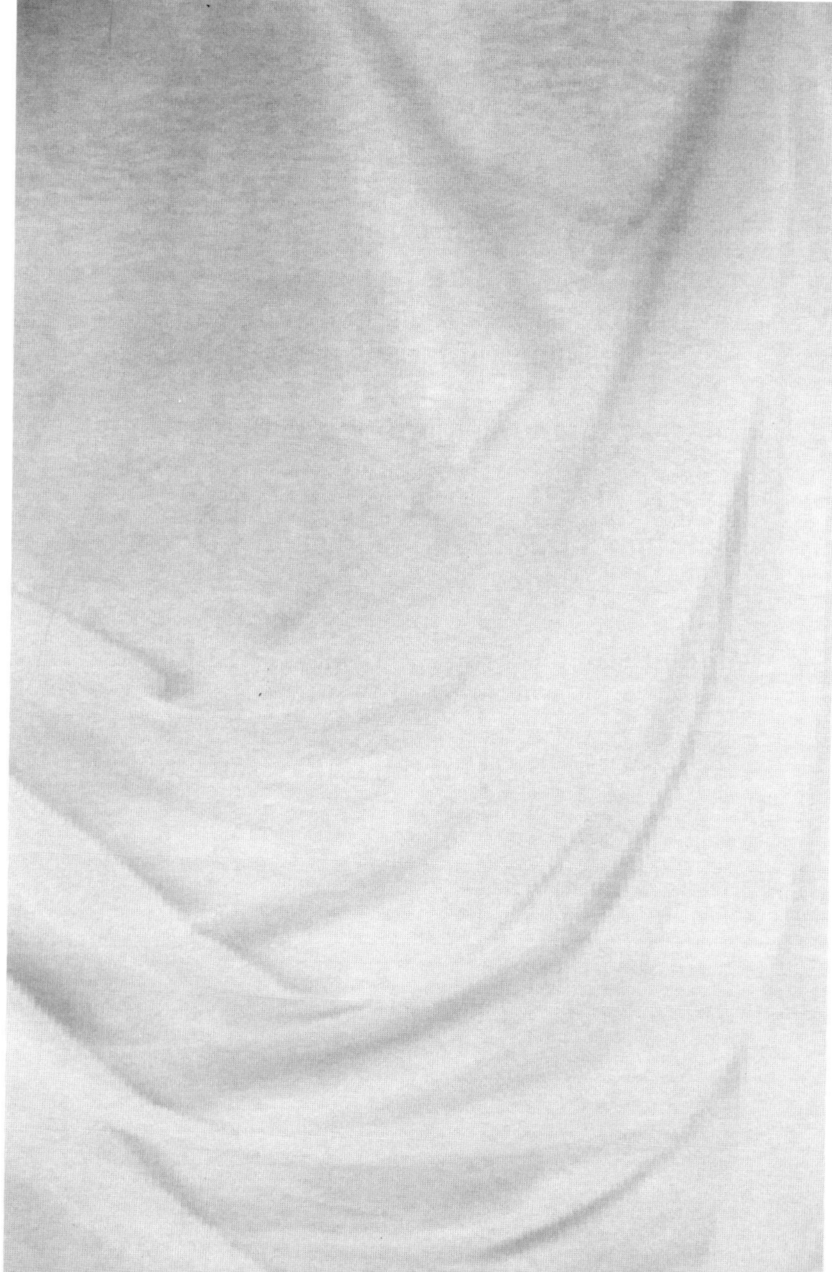

Understanding Men

A woman marries a man, expecting she can change him…she can't.

Men wake up in the morning as good-looking as they were when they went to sleep.

Men think, dream, and talk about sex more than any other topic.

All men are good for the first year…then the warranty runs out.

Men's faults: everything they say and everything they do.

Naughty Game

#29

Take It Off...
Take It ALL Off!

It's not Avon calling!

Take It Off ... Take It ALL Off!

Here's a game only for the most adventurous woman who is ready to test her sense of confidence while gaining the utmost love of her man. You have the power to make this game as basic or as stimulating as you are comfortable with. Use your imagination to create an evening the both of you will relish for years to come, when you hire a stripper to come to your home in Take It Off ...Take It ALL Off!

Start with the basics. In the Yellow Pages of your phone book, under categories such as "Singing Telegrams" and "Entertainers," you'll find several companies who can provide what you need. When you arrange for the stripper, be very clear what you have in mind. Let them know you are hiring someone to dance for just the two of you. Perhaps, if you are on the daring side, you'd like to have the stripper show you some moves, so you can imitate her after she has gone. Many strippers will undress only as far as a bra or pasties and a thong. Discuss your preferences ahead of time.

Plan for the evening by setting a mood that will make you comfortable and enhance the experience. Arrange for music of your own for after she has gone (she will bring her own.) Consider your outfit if you plan to dance with her. Fill the room with incense. Would candlelight be better or do you want all lights blazing? Whatever your choices, you can be sure that your lover will be so enthralled by your daring act that he will love every minute of the performance, as well as the encore you and he will provide later that night alone.

Prepare yourself by taking a long, luxurious bath, fragrant with your favorite scent. Caress yourself, enjoying every curve, the touch of flesh on hot flesh. Sip a glass of wine to spread warmth throughout your body in anticipation of the evening you have so carefully arranged. Greet your man at the door, and settle him comfortably on a couch with merely a hint of the impending surprise. When your doorbell rings, kiss him sweetly, whispering "I have a surprise just for you" and let the show begin!

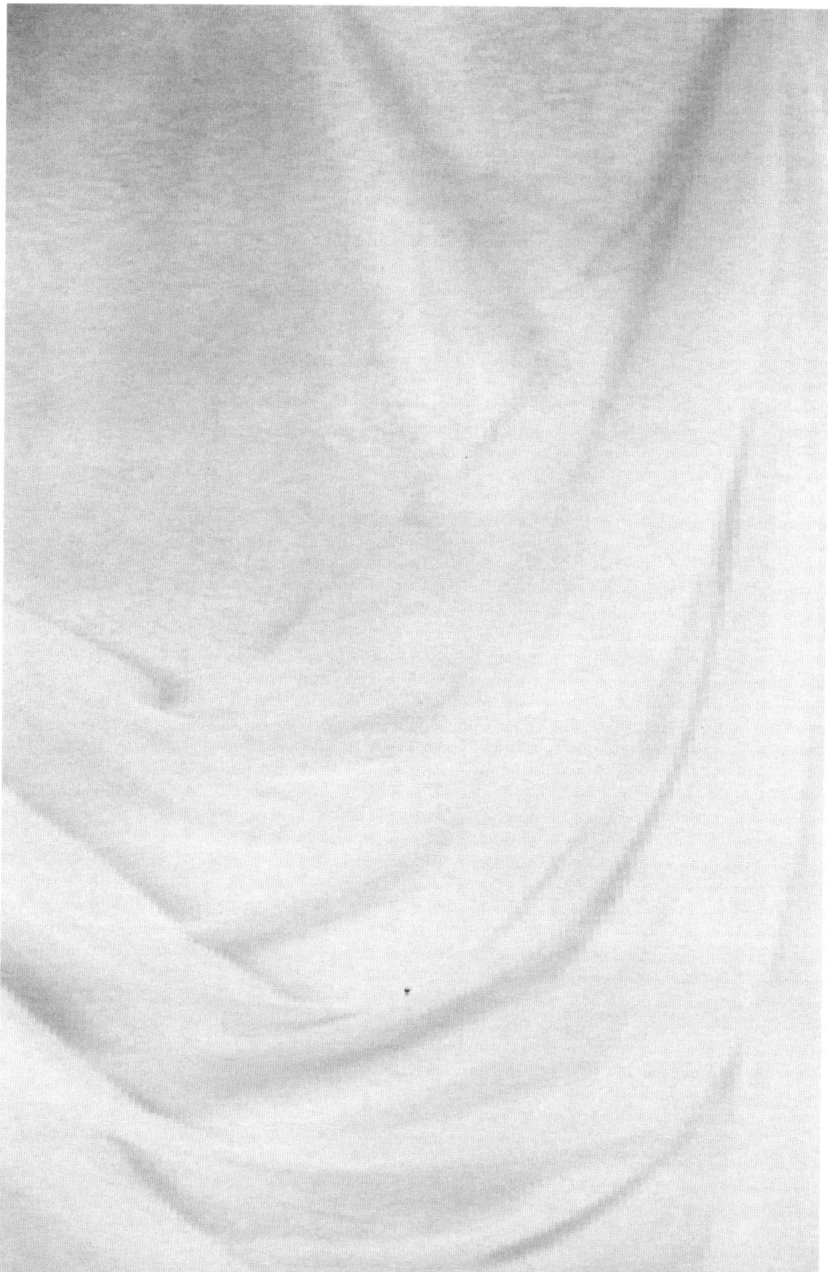

To Be United

See with your Mind
Touch with your Heart
Laugh with your Soul
Listen with Love

Naughty Game

#30

The Honey Pot

You won't want to get out of this sticky situation!

The Honey Pot

Ready for a little gooey treat, of sweet on sweet? Tonight's game will give you a sugar high matched only by the orgasmic high you'll both remember for a long time to come, when you combine your honey and The Honey Pot.

Strip the top covers, blankets and sheet from your bed leaving just the bottom sheet. Place a jar of honey on the bedside table and lure your lady into the bedroom. Slowly and methodically, remove her clothing, then place her in the middle of the bed on her back. Standing at the foot of the bed, arouse her with the visual treat of watching you undress, your dick already hardening with the anticipation of the sweets in store for you both.

On your knees, straddle her and reach for The Honey Pot. Open the jar and dip your fingers inside. Lick your fingers clean, one at a time, while keeping your eyes locked with hers. With more honey on your index finger, trace her mouth gently, letting her suck the nectar you offer. Continue finger dipping into the pot then touching her body to deposit the sweets. Start with her tits, covering her nipples with the sticky substance, then obligingly licking them clean with firm, thorough strokes of your tongue. Watch her nipples become rock hard as she arches for more. Continue down her belly, leaving a trail of honey for you to nibble away. Spread her labia and paint a thin coating on her clit and slit, which, of course, you must now clean up for her. Let your tongue dance over her pussy and deep inside her until she comes, savoring the mixture of honey with her own sweet juices.

Now, move up alongside her to position your cock near her hungry mouth. Let her reach into The Honey Pot to be able to slather your throbbing member with sweetness before engulfing you with her wet, hot mouth. As she sucks you clean, she'll also suck you dry when you explode between her lips in sheer ecstasy.

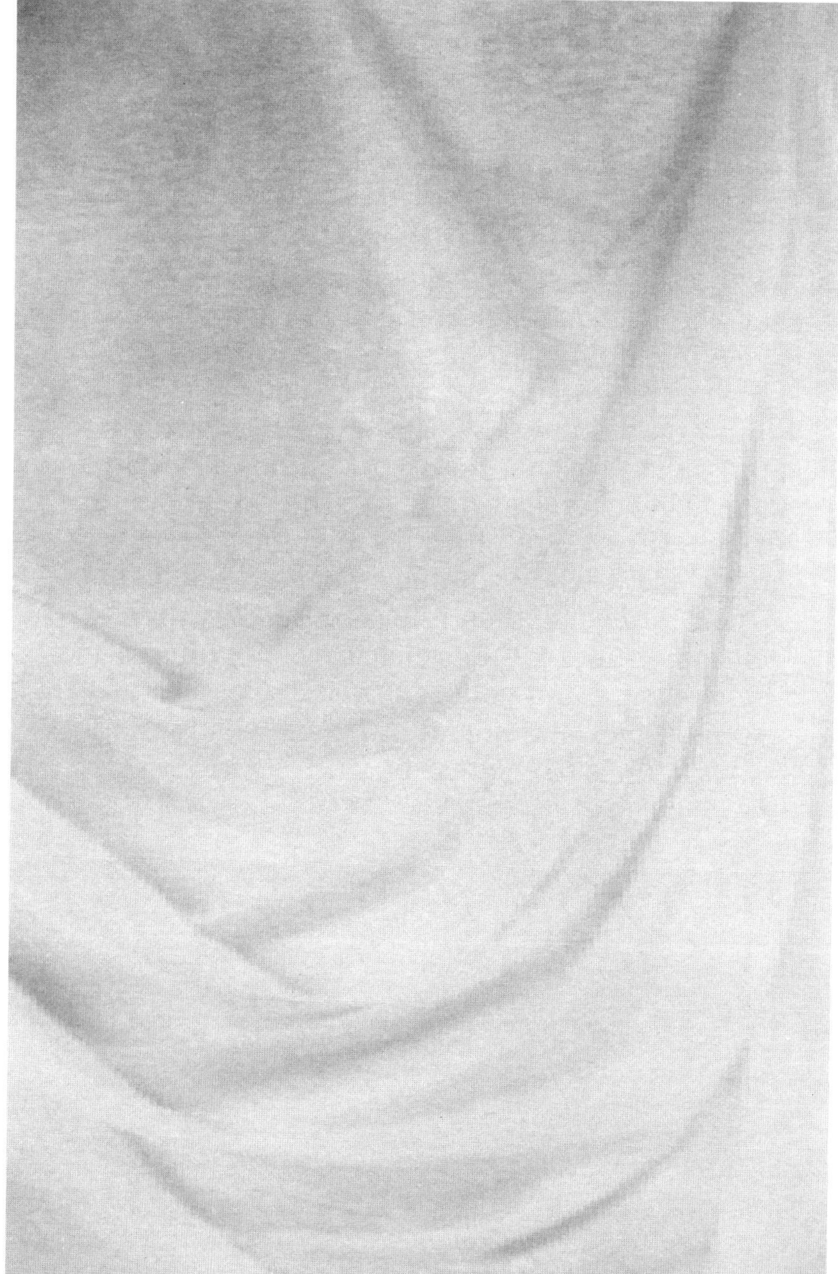

Forget the Gym!

Ladies, do you spend time at the gym, lifting weights, doing aerobics, cycling for hours to firm and tighten every muscle you have, and some you didn't know you have? NEVER forget the most important muscle you possess! Do your kegel exercises daily – in the car, standing in line, sitting in a business meeting and, most importantly, while you have his hot cock inside you! Squeeze, then release; squeeze, then release; squeeze, then release! You'll intensify his pleasure and your own. He'll worship the ground you walk on and overlook what gravity does to the rest of your body!

Naughty Game

#31

The Biggest Vibrator
Ever Made

Take your love life
for a spin!

The Biggest Vibrator Ever Made

Many women have learned to enjoy a little extra stimulation with the use of a vibrator, whether they are having solo sex or as an aid to foreplay with their man. But until you play with The Biggest Vibrator Ever Made, you've missed the jolt of your life!

Have a big blanket that needs washing? Or several oversized towels? Yes, your every day washing machine is just the ticket to rock your socks, while cleaning them too! The heavier the load in the washing machine, the more vibrating action you'll get as it spins those water-laden items.

Place your heaviest items in your washing machine, and be ready yourself - perhaps nude with just a towel or robe to cover your bare essentials. Call to your lover to bring a towel from the bathroom to add to the load. When he appears, unveil yourself and help him strip down to nothingness before he seats himself atop the machine. Kneel facing him, straddling his cock which will become agitated and ready for you long before the machine itself starts agitating! Ease your wet pussy over his shaft, encasing him in your warmth. Hold him tight, flexing your love muscle until the machine starts spinning and vibrating. Feel the movement and go with it. Make small little circles, swirling him inside you as the washing machine spins. As the machine pauses to drain, pause too, gaining energy for the coming momentum of the spin cycle. Vibrations will increase both inside and out as the washing machine spins itself crazy, taking you both along to an exhausting and happy ending - a great workout and good, clean fun to boot!

One added benefit to this game? If you've ever had trouble getting your lover to help with the laundry, one spin aboard The Biggest Vibrator Ever Made will change his attitude forever!

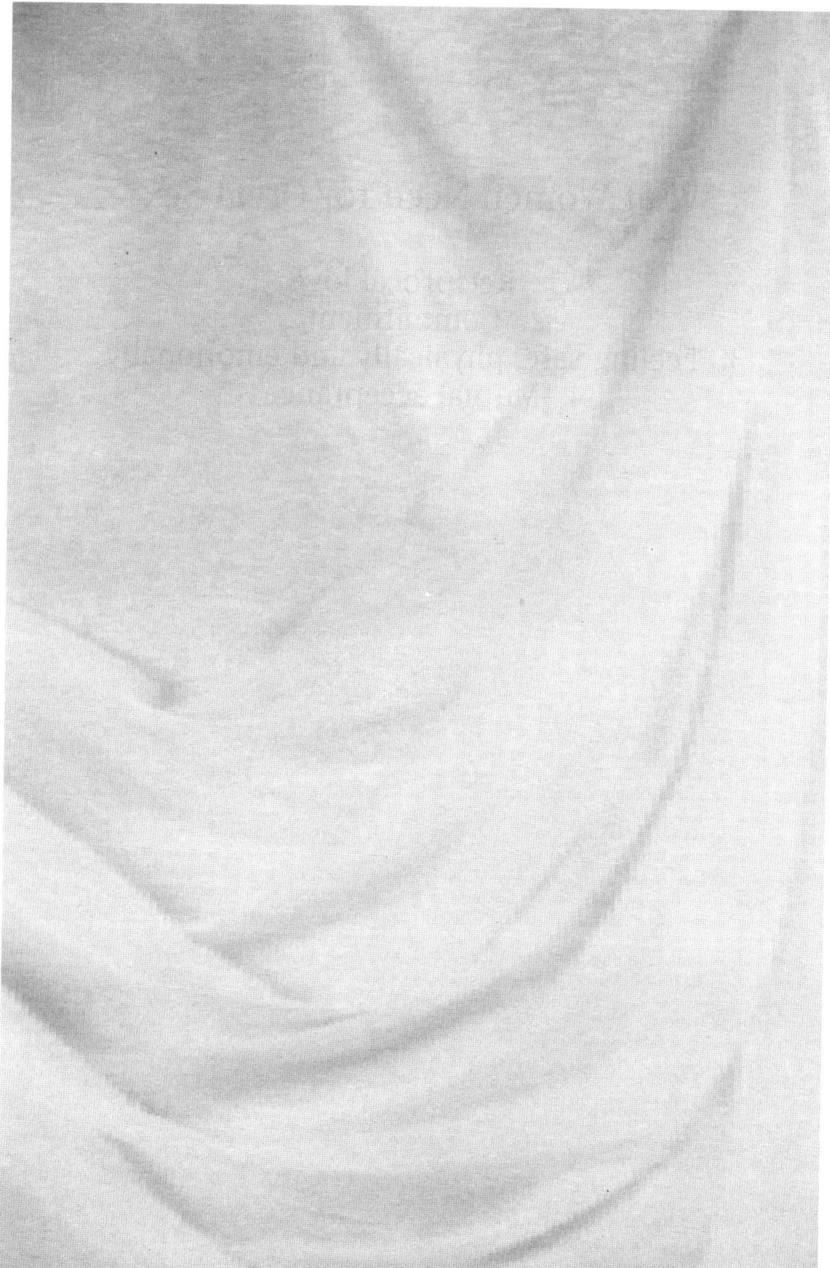

What Women Need for Great Sex

1. Reciprocal love
2. Commitment
3. Feeling safe, physically and emotionally
4. Mutual acceptance

Naughty Game

#32

Sex Education

You're guaranteed
an A+ in this course!

Sex Education

Who says learning can't be fun? No matter how much you think you know, a little refresher class and lab work can go a long way to increase your knowledge and skill. Tonight you are going to play school, and every good teacher knows that visual aids are a must to engage a student's interest and participation.

To prepare for class, all you need is one good adult film. You can easily rent one, or most cable television companies have a variety of choices which you can access by a simple telephone call. Have paper and pencils handy, for note taking, because you both will have a test to take when the film is done.

Tell your lover to jot down notes during the movie of all the activities she sees that most titillate her. You will do the same. No fair cheating by peeking! Watch for ways the actors use their hands and their mouths that are different from things you've tried before. Listen for the ways they excite each other with moans or sighs, the words they use to urge each other on. Notice the different positions of their bodies as they join together in sexual bliss.

When the movie is finished, exchange notes with your lover. While you read the things that excited her, she will be reading the notes you made about what turned you on the most. Now comes the test and your bedroom is the laboratory of sexual experiments!

Take turns practicing what you have just learned - not just from the film, but from the notes you both made. Read aloud the first item from her list, then imitate it. Ask her how you did; let her show you how to get an A+. Next she will read and then imitate one of the scenes that got you all hot and bothered. As much as you think you know about each other, you'll both be surprised by how much more you can still learn. Practice makes perfect, and there are few subjects that people are willing to study as hard as they do when they take Sex Education.

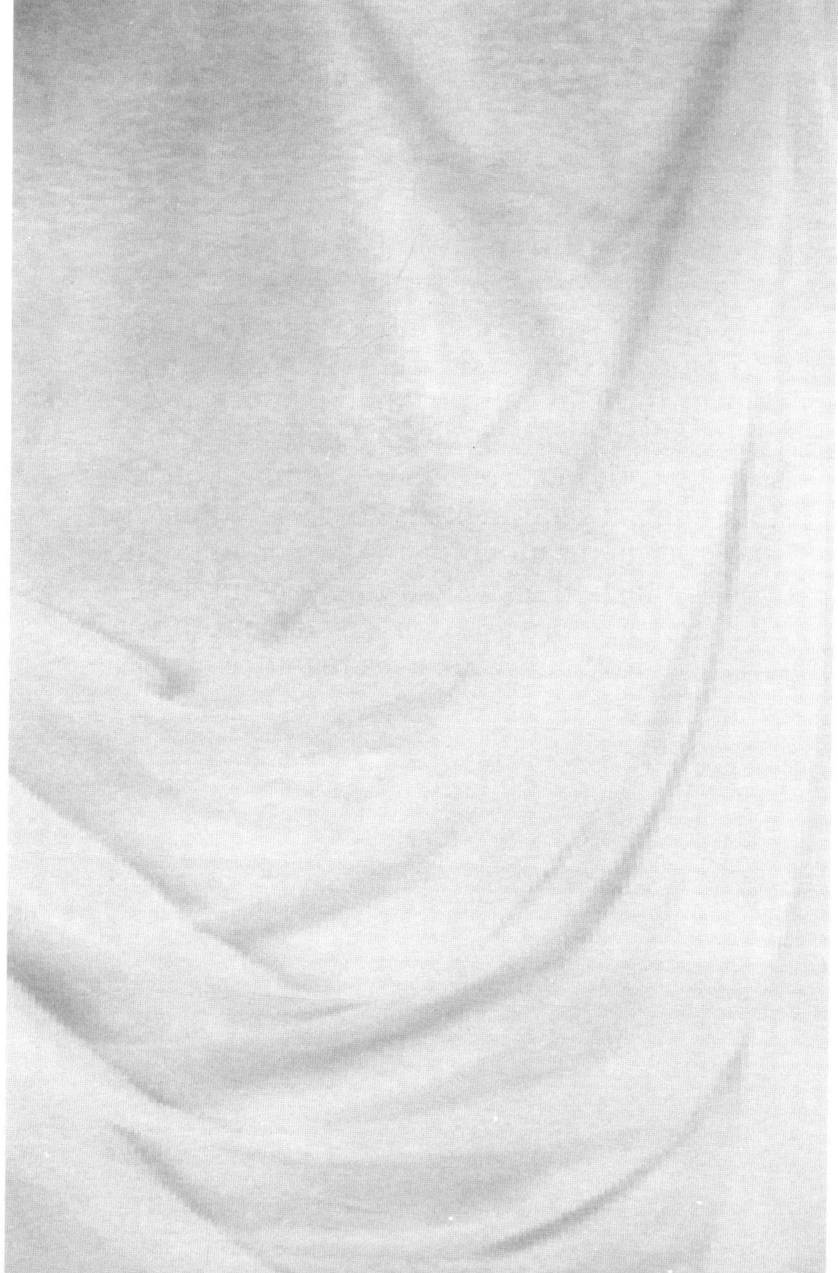

Build a Time Capsule

Capture your love, your memories, your treasures, your secrets, and your past to put away for your future. Build a time capsule together! Collect old love notes, favorite sayings, a flower from your wedding, your first love song, a sentimental photo – anything that has special meaning for the two of you. Tuck your collection on a shelf to bring out, review, add to and store away as a testament to your love and your lives together.

Naughty Game

#33

Phone Home

ET would never have been left behind!

Phone Home

A fun and fantastic way to please your man and drive him wild is to Phone Home and talk dirty to him. Phone sex is an enormous turn-on for a lot of people. You can use your voice as a sex tool, while describing things you might not take the time to say when together. Phone sex builds anticipation, and allows your imaginations to fuel the passion of lusting after each other.

You decide when and where it is best to follow through with this game. You might want to play with his mind at work, teasing him at a time and place where he is limited to act out his responses. Or you may choose to run a quick errand after dinner tonight, calling him from the corner pay phone. Use your huskiest, sexiest voice; the softer you talk, the more he will strain to hear, giving you his undivided attention. Caress each word as you paint a vision of your desires, while building his:

"Hey, baby! I just had to hear your voice. I was thinking about you, missing you, and suddenly wanting you. It's like you're here, pressing up against me. I can feel your hands on my tits, pinching my nipples to make them stand at attention for you. I'm rubbing them hard, pretending it's you. I just felt this incredible surge through my pussy. It's all wet and hot and throbbing. I'm standing here, touching myself because I want you inside me. I've got my legs spread and my fingers are playing with my clit. It's so hard and ready. If I close my eyes, I can picture you coming toward me with your cock all big and wet and juicy. I want it in my mouth, licking you all over like a big lollipop. Touch yourself, baby. That's it, nice and firm, the way I like to hold you and feel you. Stroke it for me, baby. Faster. Harder. I've got my fingers inside me now, wiggling around, my thumb on my clit, and I'm dripping for you. Come for me, baby. Come. I'm coming now, o-o-oh...can you feel it? Can you feel the walls of my cunt clasping your cock, sucking every last drop from you? I want you, baby. You're mine!"

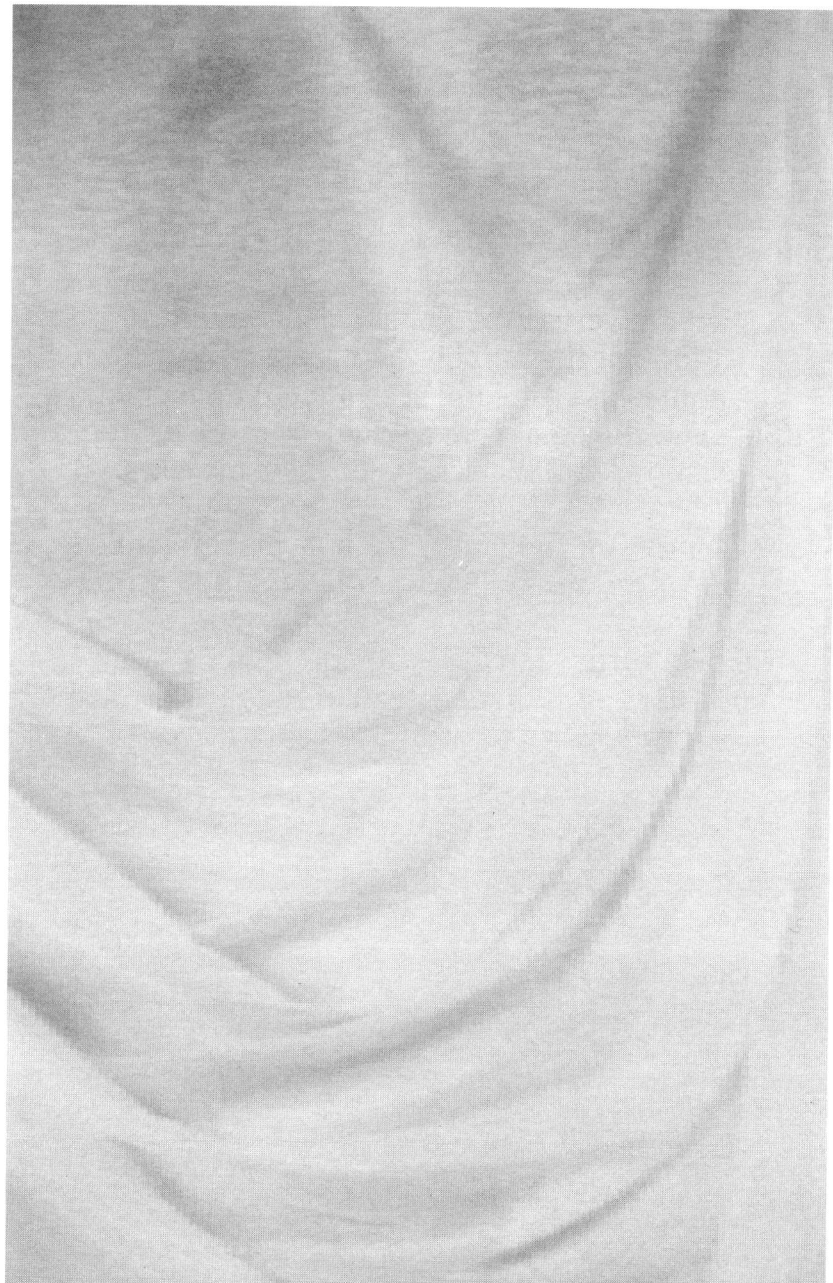

Know and Respect the Differences

Men are very turned on by visual stimuli – just look at the number and variety of men's magazines of erotic images. Men like the lights on when they make love. They want to see the reactions and the results of their prowess!

Women want to hide! They fear performance pressure. They want lights out!

So take turns! Loving is all about giving what your partner wants, instead of only what you want.

Naughty Game

#34

Arts And Crafts

A night of "fine" art!

Arts And Crafts

Many people consider the human form to be a work of art, appreciating the differences and reveling in knowing every contour of their lover's shape. Today's game will provide a whole new avenue of exploration, turning your bodies into canvasses on which to draw and paint and scribble to your heart's content, only to be easily washed away to begin again.

You already possess the "reusable canvasses." All you need to play is a variety of paints, pens and crayons. While you can invest in costly body paint sold at adult and novelty shops, acrylic paints found in hardware, toy, or drug stores are safe, non-toxic, and washable. To add further interest to the artwork, purchase some dry erasable pens in various colors, the kind used on erasable memo boards. Lastly, if you wish, try some of the made-for-the-bath crayons. Place all your supplies on the bathroom counter and invite your lover to join you for an evening of Arts And Crafts.

In front of the bathroom mirror, help her to disrobe, admiring the texture of her skin, its nuances and markings. You needn't be a Picasso or a Rembrandt to enjoy the pleasures of this kind of Arts And Crafts. Bring forth your curiosity, childlike innocence, and imagination to create a body of art. Draw eyelids around her nipples and line them with lashes. Perhaps her butt cheeks will become Siamese Twins. Her spine could be the trunk of a beautiful tree leafing out across her shoulders. Human "imperfections" - moles, scars, veins - can be incorporated into your drawings, making light of them. When you have finished, give her a turn to play artist. Then jump in the shower together and scrub your canvasses clean, making them new to begin again - although you might need to wait for another day. This kind of Arts and Crafts is so stimulating you are likely to find it tempting to experiment with brush strokes of a different kind. You'll have one giant paintbrush ready to make its mark, leaving your own, very personal signature behind.

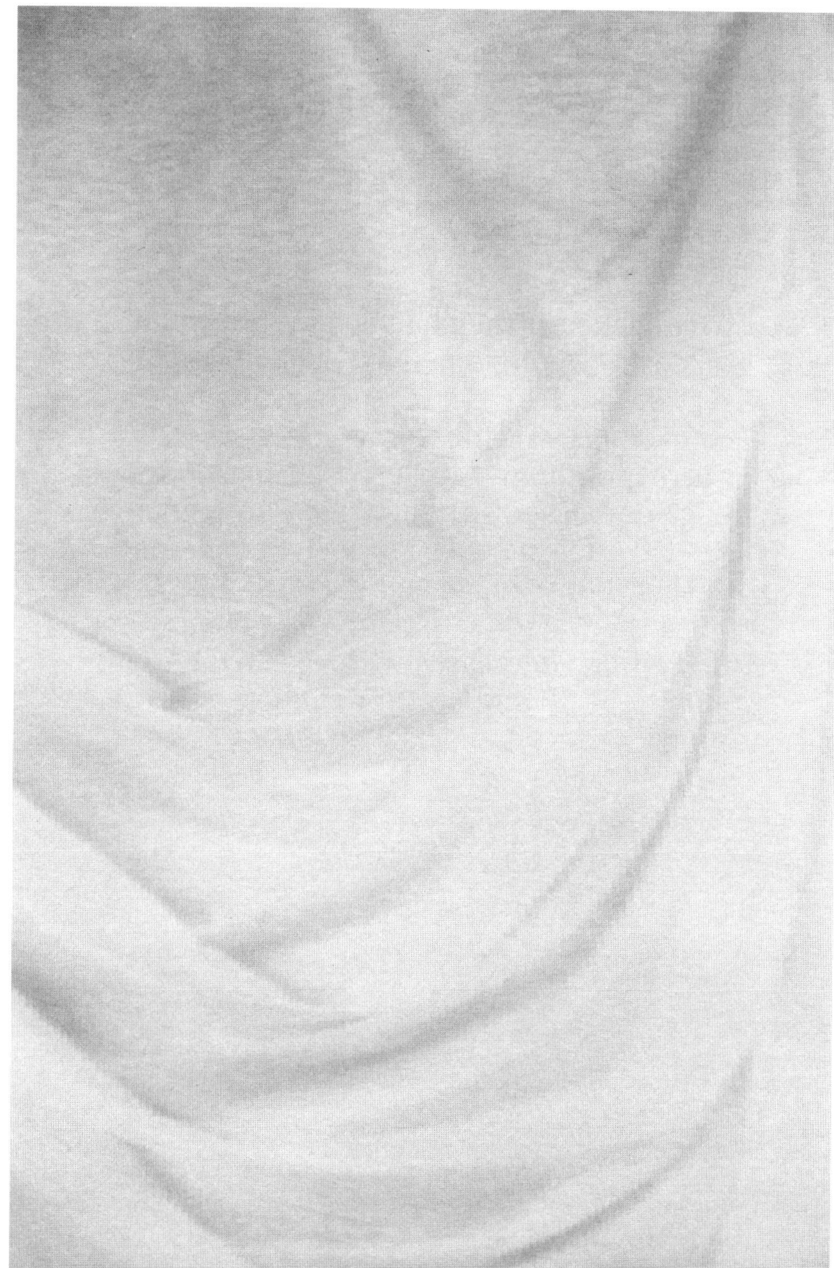

As Women Age

When asked if they had achieved sexual ecstasy, 85% of women aged 20 - 30 said yes. That increased to 89% for women 30 - 40 and 91% for women over 40. Correspondingly, anxiety over her body image decreased with age. 63% of women 20 - 30 and 30 - 40 report that concerns with their body image and performance gets in the way of satisfying sex. That percentage decreases with age! 51% for women 40 - 50 and 46% for women over 50.

Naughty Game

#35

Kisses From The Heart

Sugar and spice
and everything nice!

Kisses From The Heart

Tonight's game will satisfy even the hungriest appetite for sweets, with your luscious body being the delectable prize! All you need are several bags of Hershey's chocolate kisses, for you will be using them to lay a trail of Kisses From The Heart.

Allow enough time to prepare both yourself and the magical trail of candy. Soak in a warm bubble bath, listening to romantic music, reveling in the anticipation of the evening you have planned for your lover and yourself. When fully relaxed, wrap yourself in a large, fluffy towel and set about creating a follow-the-kisses pathway that will lead your lover from the front door, through the house, and ending at the foot of your bed. Then create the shape of a huge heart out of candy kisses atop your bed. Leave a note in a basket at the front door that reads, "I've scattered kisses, my love, for you to follow until they bring you truly home. I'm waiting for you at the end of your hunt, anxious to eat our way together toward a sweet finale!"

Position yourself on your bed, inside the heart of chocolate, completely naked except for a few, strategically placed, unwrapped candies - one atop each nipple, one inside your navel, and another squeezed between the lips of your pussy.

When you hear your lover enter the house, relax, placing your hands laced behind your head, allowing your full form to be majestically stretched out awaiting him. When he enters the room, smile ever so slightly and reach your arms outward in a welcoming gesture. Tell him, "Darling, I've been longing for your kisses all day." Guaranteed, he will soon be sweeping the extra candies from the bed as he melts into your arms, hungry to eat his sweet little surprises - and you!

And in the future, whenever you want to bring a special smile to his face and a glint to his eye, all you'll have to do is whisper, "I want to give you Kisses From The Heart!"

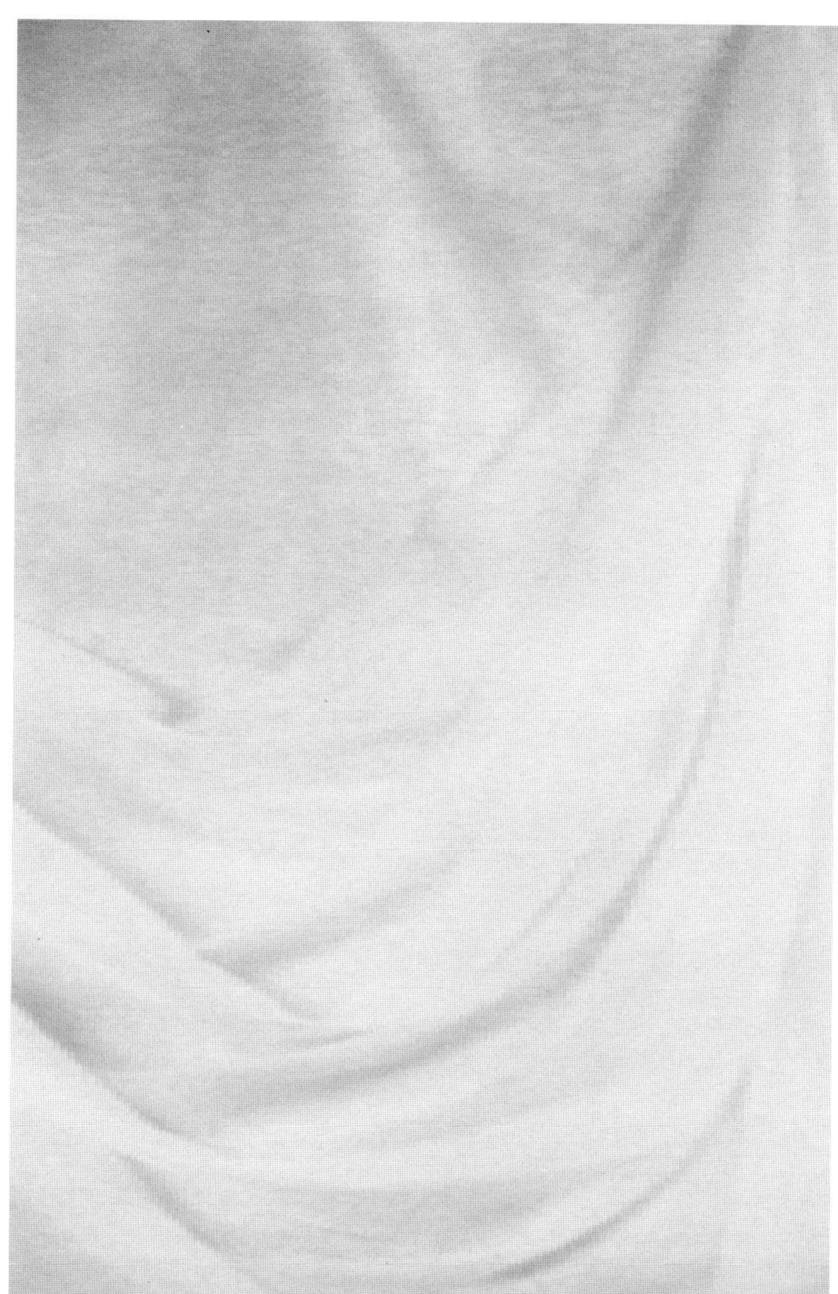

Should We Or Shouldn't We?

46% of men surveyed and 34% of women say that some form of soft pornography is a regular prelude to their passion play.

Naughty Game

#36

Love in the Backseat

Go back to the future!

Love in the Backseat

Remember the days when your opportunities to make love were sometimes limited by not having any privacy? So many couples learned the art of acrobatics when they found a nice, quiet place to park the car and would crawl in the backseat to enjoy a few stolen minutes of bliss.

For couples who have been together awhile and have a home together, the routines of sex often become limited to the same place, the same time and the same way. Making Love in the Backseat carries with it a great deal of nostalgia for most people, and chances are you may never have enjoyed this particular adventure with your current lover. So this game will provide the ticket for an advanced reenactment - by making love in the back seat of a limo!

Every woman deserves to occasionally be treated like a Queen. Set aside an evening and tell your lover only that she must be ready at a certain time for a fancy evening on the town. Limousine rentals are often packaged with a three hour minimum. It pays to shop around, comparing not only cost but amenities. Most limos are equipped with a bar, a phone, TV, CD player and moon roof. More extravagant models even come with their own hot tub. But a privacy partition is your most important need, as you'll want the driver's eyes on the road, not on the two of you.

Plan ahead for the evening by delivering your favorite CD's, a bottle of wine, perhaps some flowers, and a basket of crusty bread, fruit and chocolates to the limousine rental office, so they may stock the car for you before arriving at your door. Pre-plan a leisurely route for the driver to take, one that will leave you free to attend to matters at hand without interruptions.

Escort your lady to the car, open her door, and settle her inside this lap of luxury on wheels. When she asks where you are going for the evening, tell her "back in time" to share a moment of bliss, capturing memories and making more, as you make Love in the Backseat!

Do Something Different!

Breaking your routine is what it's all about!

Buy a Wonderbra
Try a temporary body tattoo
Switch to a garter belt and hose
Order body jewelry (waist chains are sexy)
Out with the flannel, in with silk and satin

Naughty Game

#37

Lap Dance...
The Last Dance Of Love

Sway to the beat of his racing heart...

Lap Dance...The Last Dance of Love

Dancing is one of the most subtle, publicly appropriate forms of foreplay known to man. But it is generally most known, and enjoyed, by women. What your man wants is a lustful, erotic expression of your passion for him. So tonight, you are going to arouse his interest, as well as other parts of his body, by performing a very personal, targeted Lap Dance...The Last Dance of Love!

Lap dancing is an art, one that you will learn herein to perfect and execute in order to bring the man in your life to a heightened sense of sexual arousal and climax. The only prop you need is music - something hot and sexy that makes you feel like moving to the pulsating beat. Once you feel the beat, you'll transmit all your energy into feeling sexual, acting sexual, and being a truly sexual entity.

There are two main elements to a lap dance. First, you must have a compliant recipient who is willing to remain seated as he receives his gift. The only rule he must follow is "No touching!" Make sure he knows and accepts this! The second element is YOU! Your attire is simple. Wear sheer-to-the-waist hose, a thong or bikini panties, and very high heels. Nothing above the waist. Keep it simple. Make him desire you - your body, your tits, your swaying secrets.

Dim the lights, hit the music! Pause, go slowly. This isn't a time to rush, even if you feel self-conscious. Listen to the music, feel it, allow your body to pick up the rhythm. As you inhale the beat, let go and let your hips follow. As they rock to the pulse, thrust your breasts forward, press them toward his face, lowering them to brush against his chest, then pull away to tantalize. Straddle his lap, gyrate to the beat, grinding your pelvis into his. Stand up, turn around and sit on him backwards. Lean into his body. Again pull away, lick your lips, and continue pulsing to the tunes till his heat becomes overwhelming. The "No touching" rule will soon be forgotten because his hands will be wanting to ravish you as you perform a Lap Dance... The Last Dance of Love!

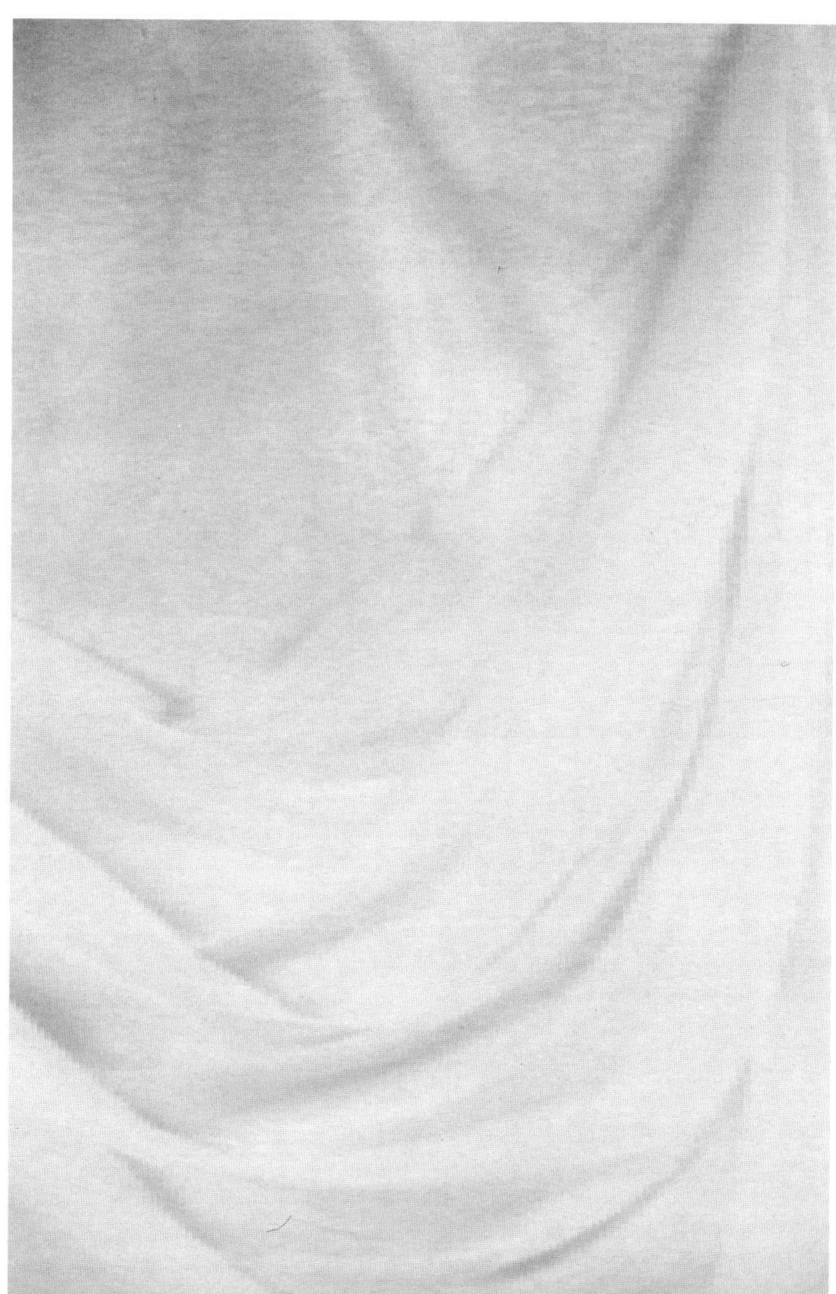

Nicknames for Breasts

The Pointer Sisters
Pom-Poms
Golden Nuggets
Mounds of Joy
Pleasure Pebbles

Naughty Game

#38

The Forbidden Zone

You'll be
"stalling" for pleasure

The Forbidden Zone

A lot of women feel a great deal of curiosity and even titillation at the thought of entering the private sanctuary of a man's public restroom - The Forbidden Zone. Few have had the chance to visit one, although many would like to be able to say they had. Tonight you are going to take your woman to The Forbidden Zone, and while you're there, treat her to a little show of your affection. You'll double her pleasure, double her fun by doubling her chances of getting caught doing something naughty!

Choose a favorite restaurant and make late night dinner reservations. This way there will be fewer patrons who may be needing the facilities. Ask for a table that you know will be within eyeshot of the restrooms. You'll need to plan your foray into The Forbidden Zone carefully - it's one thing to <u>risk</u> getting caught; another to take careless chances.

Either after ordering your meal, or between courses, when you are sure the men's room is unoccupied, take your lover by the hand and tell her to follow you. She may resist when you approach the men's room door, but will feel a rush of heady excitement when you pull her into the room. Guide her toward one of the stalls, and lock the door behind you. Shush her giggles and help her to remove her shoes before standing her up on the seat, facing you. This way no one who may enter will notice that you have a woman trapped in the stall with you!

Now you are face to face with sweet pussy for the eating. Have her brace herself by placing both hands on the walls of the stall. Remove her hose, then her panties. Caress her, seeking the feel of wetness that signals her excitement. Let your middle finger probe her insides, while your thumb plays gently with her throbbing, enlarged clit. With your other hand, stroke her butt cheeks, squeezing them in rhythm to the throbbing you are feeling at this moment. Bend forward to kiss, then lick and eat her to a frenzied finish - in The Forbidden Zone!

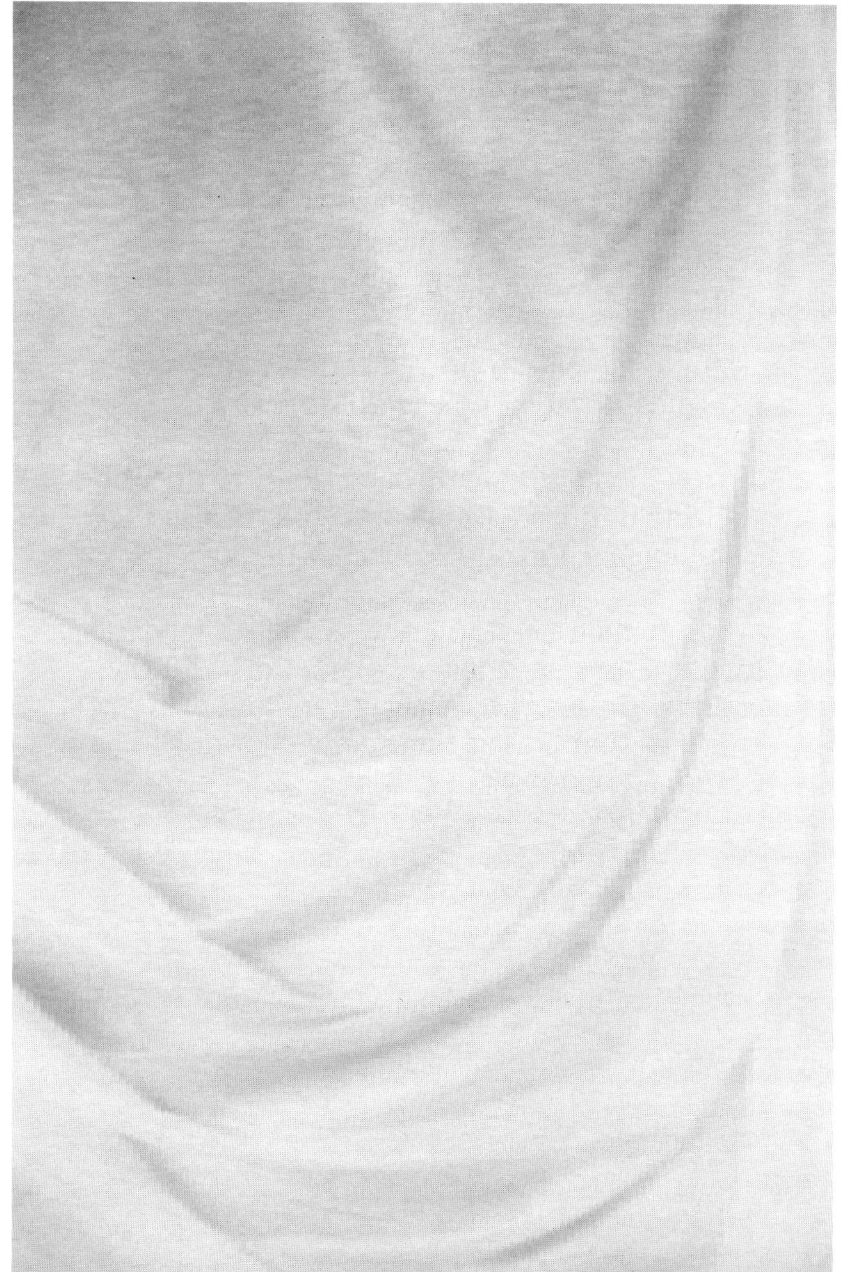

Take It or Leave It
But You Can't Change It!

Single men are reported to have solo sex (masturbate) one to two times a day.

Married men still masturbate! Reportedly only one to two times a week, but nonetheless they still engage in self-pleasuring themselves.

What women need to know is that this is no reflection on their man's satisfaction with their sex life with their life partner. In fact, most say they are thinking of their beloved, not some fictional creature! So accept it, even offer to help, but don't take it personally!

Naughty Game

#39

The Honey-Do List

Let the "Master Craftsman" strut his stuff!

The Honey-Do List

Every couple has projects at home, forever waiting to be done. Many women create a special Honey-Do List - things they need their lover to help take care of. This game is a sure-fire way to enlist his utmost cooperation!

Regardless of what chores are really on your list, tell your lover that the two of you need to go to the local hardware store to purchase a few things in order to tackle some of your home projects. While most men hate the prospect of having to take care of the routine repairs around the house, they LOVE to go to hardware stores.

While shopping, going up and down the aisles, be sure to put the following items into your cart: some rope, a roll of electrical tape, and a bright, red bandana. Tell your lover that you've just remembered one special project that really needs immediate attention as soon as you both get home.

As you are carrying your purchases into the home, be sure the three items mentioned above are taken to your bedroom. Ask him to join you in looking at an urgent problem in your master bathroom. Unaware, and probably not too enthusiastically, he will follow to see what needs to be fixed. Little does he know, it's you!

As he glances around, still wondering what the emergency is, take the bandana and wrap it around your eyes. Then hold up the rope and the tape and tell him, "Honey, I'm like a pipe ready to burst! I think you need to secure me and then rectify the situation!"

Now let the master craftsman get to work! Wriggle out of your clothes and have him bind your arms together over your head. He may need to restrain your legs, too, if they are in the way of his work. As he plunges his rod into your hole, the screams you emit will be like the steam released from a pent-up furnace.

Once he knows the rewards of helping around the house, you'll never again have any trouble enlisting his assistance with your Honey-Do List!

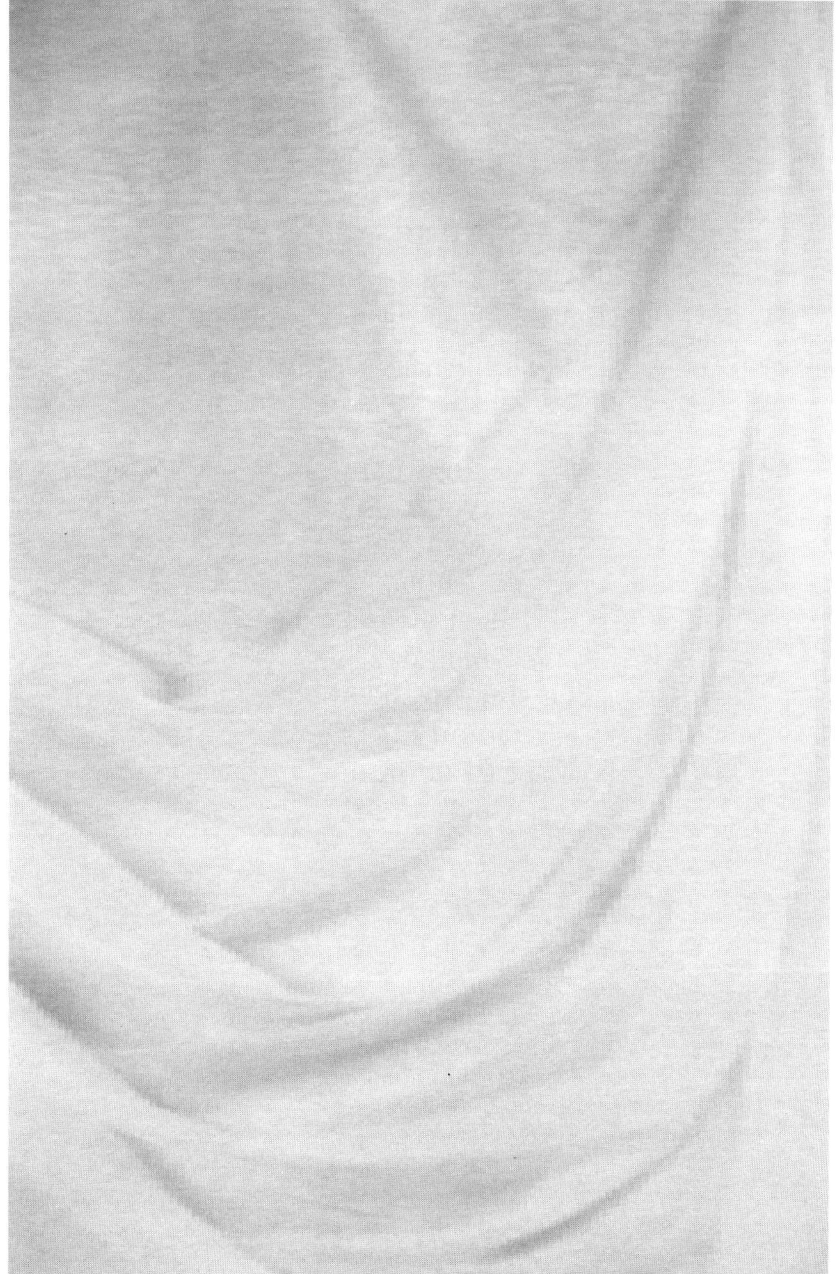

An Erotic Meal

Part of what makes a food an aphrodisiac is its erotic shape. Plan a dinner that will plant food for thought!

Consider using:
Avocados
Fresh Figs
Chiles
Black Beans
Bananas
Oysters in the Shell
Onion Rings
Ice Cream Cone
Cucumbers

Naughty Game

#40

The Exercise Instructor

Keeping fit
never felt so good!

The Exercise Instructor

Whether you and your lover are fitness fanatics or not, you may find yourselves transformed when you initiate a new work out program to exercise more than just her abs or pecks. Some muscles are even more important in the game of love, and it is your job, as The Exercise Instructor, to first test then help tone your lover's love muscles.

Clear the floor of your living room and assemble the equipment you will need. If you don't own hand weights, two one-pound cans will do. A blanket can serve as your mat. If your box of "play toys" still doesn't contain a vibrator, you can substitute a fat, raw, peeled carrot. And every good Exercise Instructor knows that a background of hot, pulsing music turns up the heat and gets everyone's juices flowing!

Strip your lover down to her bra and panties, telling her you are going to first evaluate the responsiveness of her sex muscles and do what you can to design a very special program just for her. Spread her legs to align her feet with her shoulders and place the weights in her hands. Ask her to extend her arms up over her head and hold that position for a moment. Cup each breast in one of your hands, feeling the weight of their fullness, squeezing firmly as you flick your thumbs over her hardening nipples. "Nice, very nice," you nod in approval. Slip her panties down to her ankles and move on to the next test. Slip your thumb between the lips of her pussy to check her nubbin of desire growing hard beneath your touch, while easing a forefinger into her aching, wet portal. Replace your finger with the dildo, telling her to squeeze, hold and release, repeating the motion to your count of ten. "Perfect, just perfect." Lay yourself on the floor, sliding between her legs, your own sex muscle ready to be exercised. Instruct her to kneel over you to finish the work out. Grasping her hips, lower her slowly onto your waiting cock, guiding her smoothly up and down, up and down as your love muscles join in mutual spasms of release. Keeping fit never felt so good!

What Would You Do If You Had a Penis For A Day?

Some of the women surveyed answered:

"I would measure it both ways."
"I would play with it all day."
"I would see how many donuts I could carry with it."
"I would want a big one and then I would show it to everyone."
"I would jump up and down and watch it swing all around."

And what would <u>your</u> pleasure be?

Naughty Game

#41

Let's Eat

Who says you can't
have dessert before dinner?

Let's Eat!

The act of sharing food has long been a prelude to great sex. Food stimulates all of our senses. Taste buds are tantalized. Aromas arouse us. The sight of different shapes can evoke erotic images. The feel of hot and cold and various textures add interest. And even the sounds of sucking and slurping and crunching creates intensity to the intimacy of sharing food for the body and love for the soul. Tonight you will prepare a feast for both body and soul that will give new meaning to the invitation, "Let's Eat!"

Clear off one long section of your kitchen counter and lay a soft, plush towel on its surface. Arrange a variety of sweet "condiments" next to the towel: a can of whipped cream (have you tried the chocolate flavor?), a bowl of maraschino cherries, a bottle of chocolate syrup, a can of chopped nuts, and a bunch of bananas. You may want to stock the freezer with some of his favorite ice cream too.

Just before your lover is to arrive home, shower and rinse carefully, because you are about to become the platter on which he will build the most decadent and delicious sundae of his life! Boost yourself up onto the countertop and lie in wait. When he walks into the kitchen, dropping his briefcase on the floor, exhausted from a long day at work, you'll be ready to surprise him with a buffet of gourmet delights. Spread your legs ever so slightly and gesture to the array of delights, from your quivering mound, your heaving breasts, and the surrounding toppings. Grasp the can of whipping cream in one hand and spray a circle of sweetness around your nipples, then invite him... "Honey, Let's Eat!"

As your man enjoys himself, creating a lavish dessert and eating his way through desire to climax, make sure he shares with you the sweet rewards. Get playful! Spray him with whipped cream and chocolate syrup. Use his own hard banana as a starting place. Relish the interaction of sharing the taste, smell, feel, sights and sounds of eating together!

Theory of "Connectivity"

Women need to make a connection
before they make love.
Men need to make love in order to
feel a connection.

Naughty Game

#42

Rent-A-Room

You won't be able to wipe that blush off your face!

Rent-a-Room

When looking to spice up your love life, a change of scenery is all that it takes. You don't need a long, expensive vacation - just a little ingenuity and a long lunch hour!

Plan this game for a day when you know that you both have the flexibility at work to enable you to take more than just an hour for your lunch break. If necessary, schedule a fictitious appointment and tell your lover that you'll both be needed to meet with your accountant or banker. That way you'll ensure enough time to languish in the afternoon in each others arms in a Rent-a-Room.

On your way to work, choose a convenient hotel and register for that evening. Request a check-in time of noon. Ask for two keys, keeping one for yourself. Have the other key delivered to your lover at work by courier, along with a hand-written note instructing her to meet you in the room at 1:00 that afternoon. Arrive early to attend to the final details. Order room service - a nice bottle of champagne, some light sandwiches, and perhaps some fruit salad. Arrange a bouquet of her favorite flowers on the table.

When she arrives, slowly undress her, carefully hanging her garments so she may return to work later. Offer her a chilled glass of wine and toast the spontaneity of your encounter. Take one of the flowers, tracing it gently over her face, shoulders, circling her breasts, down her belly, wiggling it between her wet thighs. Ease her gently onto the bed as you use your lips to retrace the path of the flower. Sprinkle champagne across her nipples and suck hungrily. Moisten your fingers in the nectar and insert them into her pulsing pussy. Enter her tenderly, ready to increase your momentum, driven by the demands of her cravings for you.

When she returns to her office with a blush on her face, her co-workers may very well wonder exactly what the two of you had to discuss with your accountant! The fact that you Rented-a-Room will be a special secret and memory just for the two of you!

Naughty Game

#43

Togas And Tubs

Oh Mighty Caesar,
How can I serve thee?

Togas And Tubs

The world was a much different place centuries ago, when the role of a woman was to anticipate and serve the needs of her man. Bathing was a ritual of scents, a form of cleansing the mind and body. As your prelude to intimacy, whisk yourselves away tonight to a time of Togas And Tubs.

Creating a seductive atmosphere is a vital aspect of breaking free from your routines, rekindling the flames of desire for your lover, and his for you. Transform your bathroom into a Roman chamber of romance. Start by filling the room with greenery and plants, preferably palms. Scented candles of all shapes and sizes should line the counters and surround the bathtub. Place a large, folded towel on the floor on which you will kneel. A decanter of rich, red wine and a large goblet should be waiting nearby, to warm his innards. Purchase oil for the bath: spicy Marjoram, effective in soothing and relaxing tired muscles, or the earthy fragrance of Patchouli, with its calming and rejuvenating properties. Last, but not least, to set the stage, fashion a simple toga for yourself. Take a plain white single bed sheet, drape it over one shoulder then wrap it around your body, securing it with a colorful belt or sash at your waist.

When your man arrives home, let him find you kneeling quietly beside the hot, steamy tub. Arise to offer him a sip of wine then remove his clothes. In the flicker of the candlelight, lead him into the bath and begin to wash and massage his taut shoulders and neck. Scoop water with your hands and let it drizzle down his back. Use a loofah sponge to gently scrub away the grime of the day. Stand to remove your belt, letting your toga fall to your feet as you slip into the bath behind him. Reach around and caress his chest, letting your hands drift lower until they graze his mighty sword. Press your tits against his back, allowing them to massage those muscles as your hand works its magic. His tensions will soon explode, then fade away as you both lay back, enveloped in the warmth of sated passions.

Dance The Night Away

The reason dancing is considered an act of foreplay is that it is a vertical act of a horizontal desire.

Naughty Game #44

The Gift Of Time

Special moments
for your lady love!

The Gift Of Time

This game is one of the most generous, selfless acts a man can perform for his woman. While men are easily and quickly both aroused and satisfied, a woman often requires more time and attention in reaching sexual satisfaction. Quickies are a gift for a man, but to make a woman feel truly special, you must give her The Gift Of Time.

To make the presentation of this game even more special, purchase a lovely new watch for your lover as a symbolic treasure of your intentions to please her. Before gift wrapping the watch, hand write individual notes - offers to perform a variety of foreplay activities that excite her and make her wet and willing to go to the summit with you. For example:

- "I will give you a full body massage with sensuous oils.
- "I will kiss your lips and wet your pussy with my loving tongue.
- "I will nibble your ears, your neck, your nipples until they are hard, yet tender for my touch.
- "I will bathe you in bubbles of lavender.
- "I will brush your hair, caress your face, stroke your breasts, tummy and thighs until you arch your body as an invitation for me to enter.

Wrap the notes and the watch together in a beautiful gift box. Adorn it with bows or flowers. Treat your special lady to an evening on the town and present the gift to her as you sip your after dinner coffee or liqueur.

When she opens the watch, she is sure to be delighted. But when she opens the individual notes - your Gifts of Time - her undying love and gratitude will be written on her face and read in the depths of her eyes, filled with love for you!

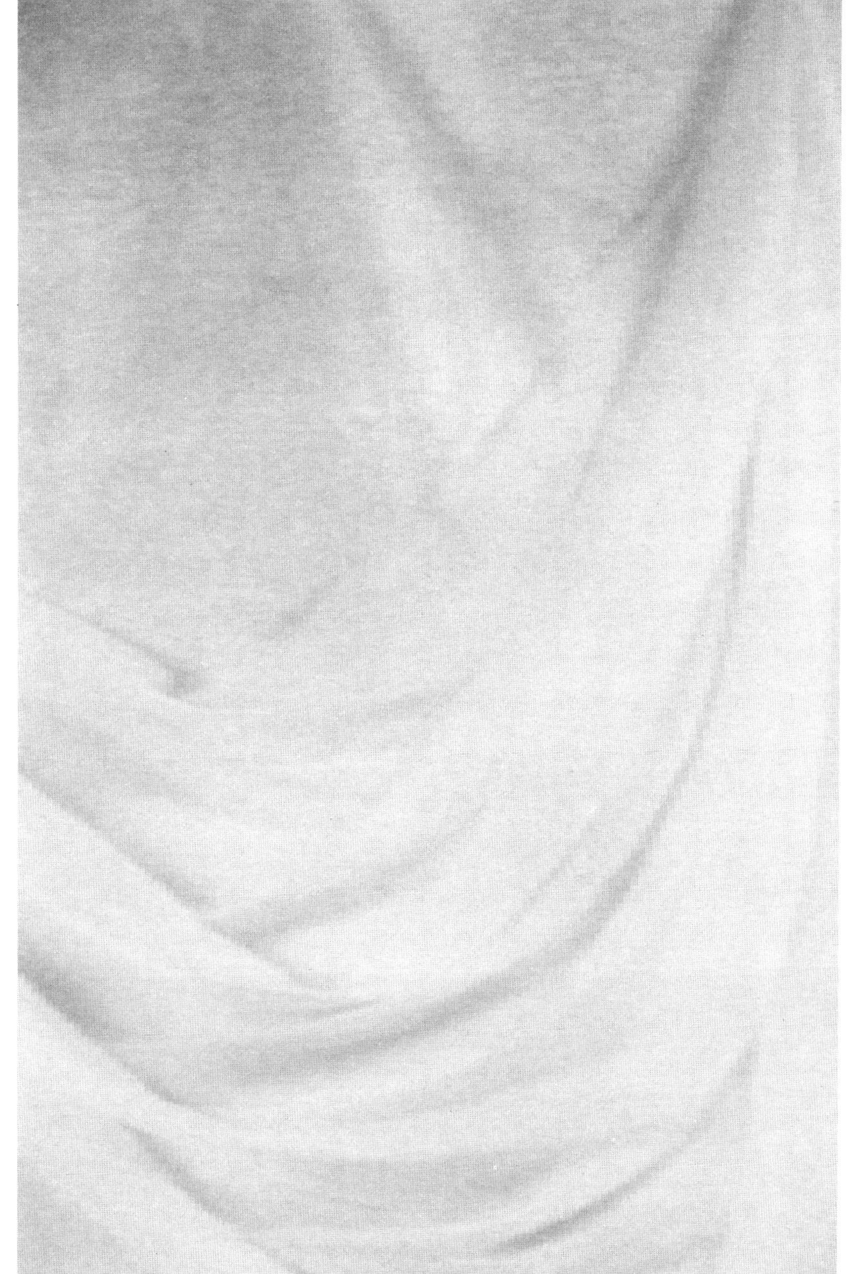

Nicknames for "The Act"

Carnal Communication
Hole-In-One
Rub the Lamp and Let the Genie Out
Slam Dunk
Kinky Kontact
Makin' Whoopee
Horizontal Tango

Naughty Game

#45

Spread 'Em

You'll need to frisk
this desperado!

Spread 'Em

One of the favorite costumes for a female stripper to wear at a bachelor party is that of a policewoman. There is something very exciting for men when they watch a woman dressed as an authority figure, acting tough, then proceed to submit to the basic animal instincts of lustful sex.

A policewoman costume is rather easily created by wearing a navy blue shirt (maybe one of his), and navy slacks (tight-fitting is best.) If you wish to be more elaborate, you could purchase a cap at a thrift shop or military supply store. A child's toy badge and holster with toy gun completes the outfit. To make the game most effective (and to add pleasure to many of your other sex games) the one accessory you need most is a pair of handcuffs, readily found at any toy store.

When your lover parks his car in the garage this evening, be ready to approach him before he enters the house. Stop him in his tracks as you issue the order, "Spread 'Em!" Have him face the car, put his hands on the roof and force his legs apart as you begin a very thorough job of frisking him. Start by patting down his arms and chest, his hips and buttocks, then move down one leg at a time before returning to his crotch for a careful "investigation." You're likely to find a hard, hidden weapon pressing against his belly! Order him to turn to face you as you remove your handcuffs from your waistband, locking them around his wrists.

Pace in front of him slowly, looking him up and down. Then begin to unbutton your shirt. "Want some of this?" you ask, as he squirms against his restraints. "You'll have to remove your weapon!" Reach toward him to caress his throbbing bulge, then unzip his pants to expose his pulsing pistol. Turn your back to him, drop your pants, and obey your own command of "Spread 'Em." As he enters you from behind, you'll know you've captured the hottest, most dangerous desperado of all time.

The Love Indicator

Clasp your hands together, lacing your fingers.
Look to see which thumb is on top!
If your right thumb is on top, pointing toward
your heart...you're a lover!
If your left thumb is on top...
you wish you were!

Naughty Game

#46

Her Pleasure Palace

Need to get back
into her good graces?

Her Pleasure Palace

The way to a woman's heart is through the gifts of romance, time, and undivided attention. Tonight you are going to create an unforgettable moment in her life when you turn your home into Her Pleasure Palace.

You will awaken and incite her sense of sight when she opens the front door to find a path of rose petals leading her into the living room, to the couch draped in a lace cloth. The room will be lit only by the soft flickering of candlelight - dozens of candles of all sizes and shapes casting their golden glow to warm her heart. You will have filled the room with the sweet aroma of her favorite incense, perfume or cologne, while soft and sexy music drifts through the air.

You will take her by the hand and lead her gracefully to her seat of honor, settling her comfortably, slipping a pillow behind the small of her back. Gently you will remove her shoes, then her hose, placing her feet into a waiting basin of warm water filled with Epsom salts. You will offer her a flute of champagne, and hand-feed her morsels of Brie and French bread, grapes, and chocolate covered strawberries. You will smooth back her hair, stroking her forehead, letting your fingers trace the outline of her nose, then her lips.

On your knees beside her, remove her feet from the basin and wrap each one in a soft, fluffy hand towel, patting them dry. Pour a dollop of massage oil into the palm of your hand, then rub your hands together briskly to warm the oil before applying it to her feet. Start with her toes, then her arch, to her heels, one foot at a time. With more oil, move slowly, firmly past her ankles to her calves, kneading and relaxing her muscles. Continue massaging her legs, moving higher and higher until you reach the summit of her mound. Slip a well-oiled finger under her panties into her waiting pussy, while using your other hand to lubricate and stroke your rigid shaft. Holding her panties aside, mount her and plunge your way home. Her Pleasure Palace has also become yours!

Gifts For The Senses

- An Aromatherapy Machine – a heat-activated device that you fill with aromatic beads, such as "Rejuvenation," "Relaxation," or "Invigoration." Fill your room with delightful scents.

- A Body Massaging Mat – whether one for the full body or just back and seat, these stimulating mats send different rates and intensities of pulsing massage.

- Sound Machine – choose from a variety of peaceful sounds, including rhythmic ocean waves, a babbling brook, a gentle spring rain, or the sultry sounds of a summer night.

Naughty Game

#47

Picture Perfect

A photo album you won't want to share!

Picture Perfect

Men are visual creatures, easily and readily aroused by photographic images. Many women feel threatened by the fear that their man is more interested in the airbrushed beauty and perfectionism displayed in countless magazines than they are by the physical attributes of the real woman at home. Not so! The reality is a man is attracted to the woman he loves, especially when she is able to convey confidence in her own unique beauty. You are going to create a photo album of Picture Perfect images of yourself that will be a lasting tribute of your love for your man and your confidence in his love for you.

If you are not already familiar with sensual photographic poses, purchase several over-the-counter magazines, such as *Playboy* and *Hustler*. Study them to determine different stances that you think would excite your lover. Pay particular attention to the scant clothing worn, the positioning of the female body, and most importantly, the lustful expressions on the alluring models.

Enlist the help of a trusted friend (or plan to use an automatic camera if you are more modest.) Arrange a time when you can have several hours of privacy to complete the needed photographic session. Using a Polaroid camera, recreate the poses you feel will most excite your lover. Ask your girlfriend to be brutally honest about what she sees in the viewfinder. Are you looking sexy? Should you rearrange a strand of hair or bend a different way? Together you are cementing your friendship as you are building an array of photographs to create a Picture Perfect memoir of your love and your lust for your lover.

Choose a luxurious leather-bound photo album, select your favorite photos, and arrange them attractively. Include a loving note from you to your lover, letting him know that this gift from you is more than Picture Perfect - it is a testament of your love and commitment to each other.

Bored?
Try These Board Games

Romantic Rendezvous
Talk Dirty to Me
Hearts are Wild
Between the Sheets
Sexual Secrets
An Enchanting Evening
The Game of Hot Seat
The Erogenous Zone Game
Intimate Commands
Strip Bingo
More Foreplay, The Game
Sensuous Exciting Experiences
Getting to Know You…Better
SeXplay

These games can be purchased at most adult sex shops or catalogs.

Naughty Game #48

You've Been So Naughty

Teach her an unforgettable lesson!

You've Been So Naughty

Sexually satisfied couples report that play-acting their favorite fantasies keeps the fun alive in their relationship. Role-playing also develops trust between a man and a woman, the number one component needed for a strong and healthy commitment. By sharing and then recreating their secret desires, they become vulnerable, opening the channels to intimate communication.

A popular theme for many is the game of schoolgirl and headmaster. Your props are simple - wear a suit and tie, and clear a desk or table of everything except a few books and a ruler. Position a chair, without arms, behind the desk.

Assemble the following on your bed for your lover - a white blouse, short skirt, knee socks, and shoes. For an added touch, tie together a few notebooks for her to carry. Include this note: "Undress COMPLETELY, then put on ONLY these four items. Put your hair in pigtails. Bring your books and report to my office immediately! The Headmaster."

Imagine the schoolgirl blush that will cross her face as she reads your commanding words. When she appears, in costume, arise from your chair, tapping the ruler against the palm of your hand. Sternly look her up and down, as you slowly pace the room, encircling her. Stop in front of her, still tapping your ruler as you say, "You've Been So Naughty! You haven't obeyed the dress code. Where is your school cap, missy? What else have you forgotten to wear?"

Using the ruler, lift the edge of her skirt. "What? No panties? You must be punished! Come with me." Lead her back to your chair and pull her down across your lap. Spank her bare bottom with the ruler, then caress the pink skin with your hands, bending to kiss its tenderness. She'll feel the rising of your own flagpole and be ready for more. Lift her to sit on the desk and rip open her shirt to expose her bare breasts. Shake your head. "No bra? Oh what am I going to do with you? You've Been So Naughty!" Lay her back on the desk and teach her an unforgettable lesson.

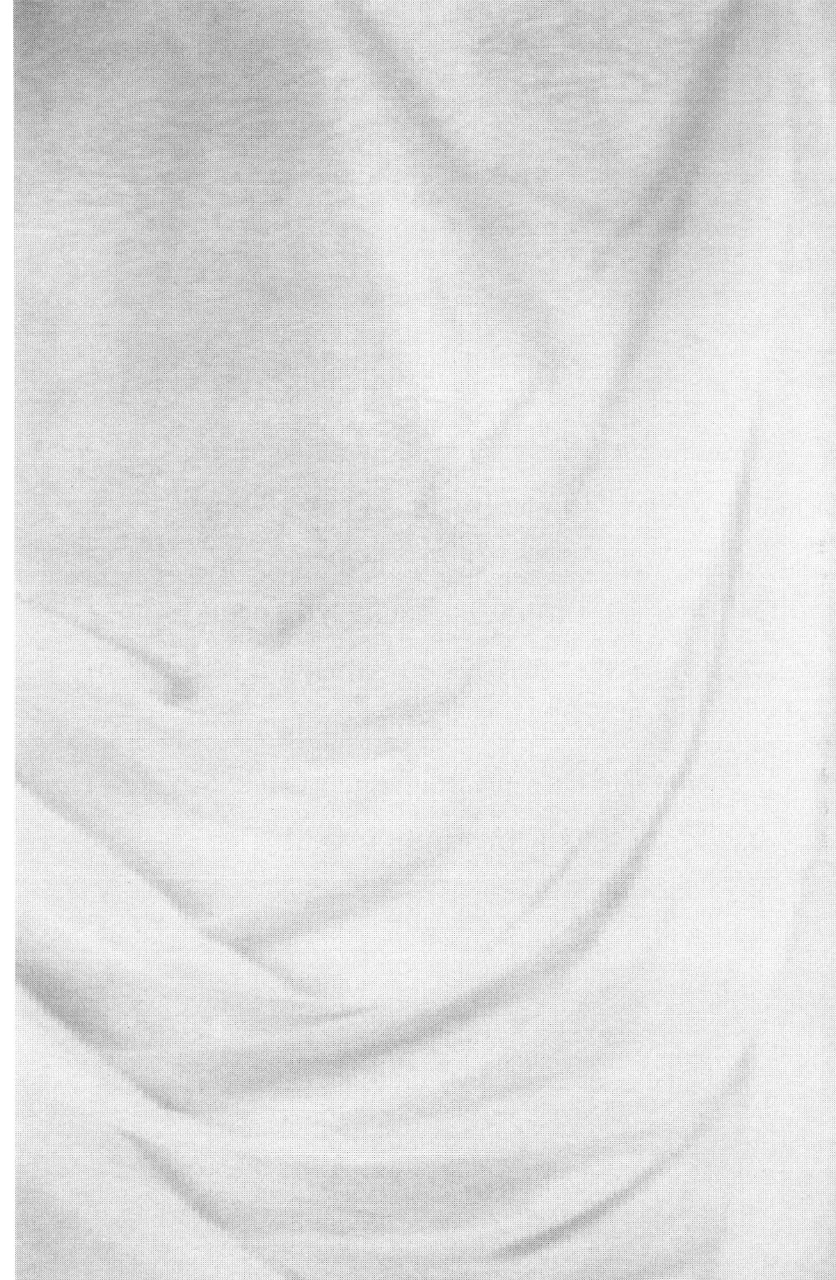

Wet and Wild Ways
To Be Playful

Wet T-shirt contests in your shower

In a public pool

Dashing through a backyard sprinkler

In the backseat of your car during a rain storm

Catch those jets in your Jacuzzi

Wash the car and hose each other down

Luxurious bubble baths

Naughty Game

#49

The Office Visit

Show him who's boss!

The Office Visit

When a man goes to work every morning, he has a mindset governed by his high levels of testosterone - identify the problem, tackle the problem, solve the problem. It's time for you to boldly invade his space to shake him up just a bit, reminding him of the real reasons he works so hard - YOU! You are going to pay him a little Office Visit.

This game works best when you take him totally by surprise. To do so, you need to be aware of his daily routine. Show some interest and find out what he has planned, so you can do some planning of your own.

Choose the day wisely, as timing is everything. After he has left for work, assemble the scanty outfit you will wear for today's adventure. A push-up bra with lacy straps and a matching pair of crotchless panties are all the basics you'll need. Accessorize simply, but be sure to wear a pair of very high heels. Cover it all with a trench coat, and you're off.

When you arrive at his place of work, make sure he is alone and enter his office. The initial surprise of seeing you unexpectedly will distract him from his duties, because you have a whole new agenda of duties he must attend to.

Stand at a distance from him, lock eyes and tell him, "Honey, there's something we must talk about - NOW!" Most men dread those very words, but you will soon demonstrate that they have a whole new meaning. Slowly and deliberately, untie the sash of your coat and let it fall open to unveil your message. If he starts to rise from his chair, order him to sit back down. Walk toward him, never allowing your eyes to leave his. Approach his chair and lean forward; have your breasts brush up against his face. Reach down to unzip his pants and extract his throbbing member. Let your body do the talking as you straddle him, easing your flesh over his, capturing his essence and bringing him to a quick and satisfying solution to his most immediate "problem." Your Office Visit will be the highlight of his day, enabling him to easily tackle anything else that may later come his way!

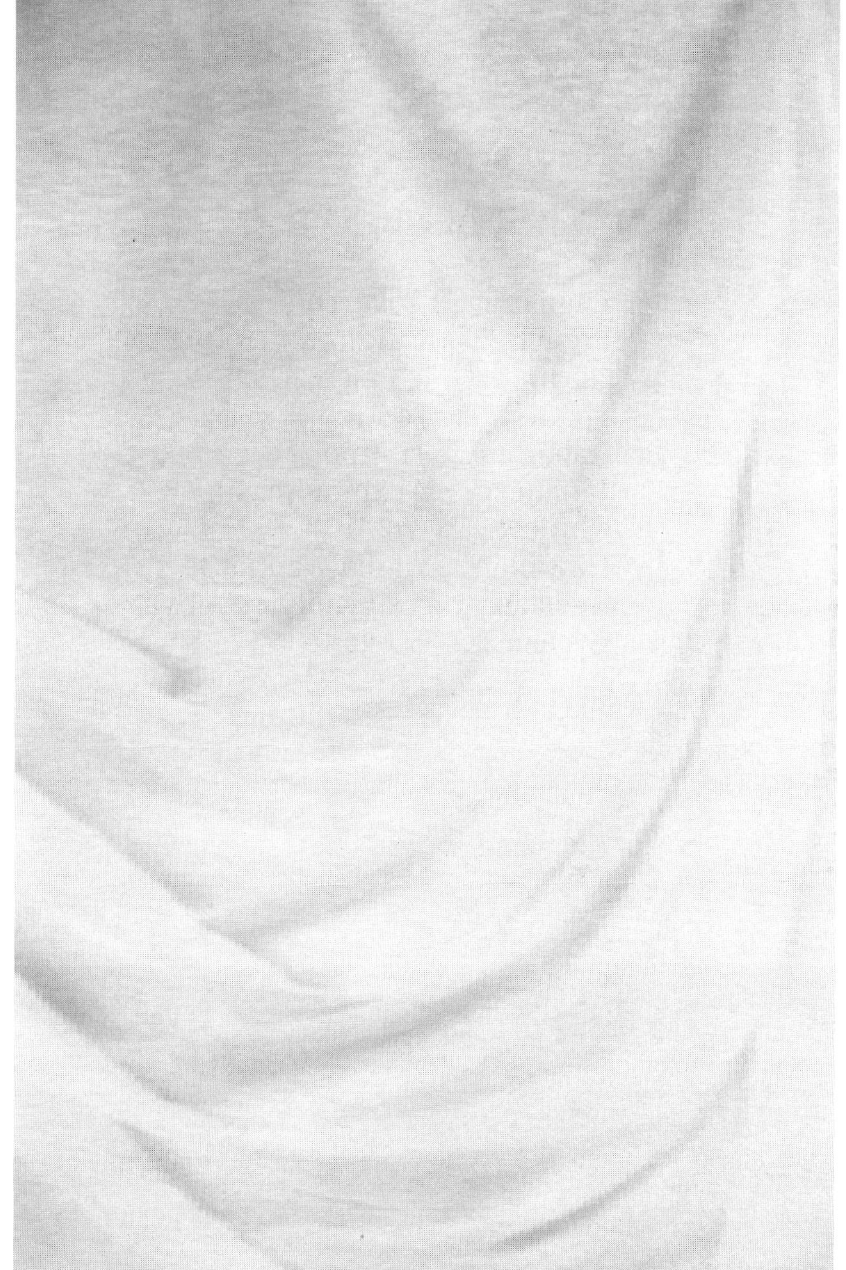

Say It Again, Sam

English……I Love You
French…….Je T'aime
German……Ich Liebe Dich
Spanish……Te Amo
Italian……...Ti Amo
Japanese…..Ai Shite Imasu
Chinese……Wo Ai Ni
Hawaiian…..Aloha Wau Ia Oe
Russian…..…Ya Lyublyu Tyebya
Greek……….S'Agapo

Naughty Game

#50

I've Been Watching You

You'll be her
"Stranger in the night!"

I've Been Watching You!

A fantasy for many is the thrill of being watched and admired from afar, inciting erotic thoughts and desires in the heart of a stranger. You are going to play the part of the "stranger" who has been worshiping your woman from afar, finally unable to control your secret passions any longer.

Type or hand-write the following message, which you will mail to her:

"**I've Been Watching You!** Last night, cloaked by the darkness of a moonless sky, I stood outside your window as you undressed. I watched you unbutton your flimsy blouse, letting it slip off your shoulders and drop unnoticed to the floor. My breath caught in my throat as you reached to unhook your bra, your taut, firm breasts bursting free of their lacy trappings. Your nipples were hard, their sweet ripeness teasing me. I licked my lips, imagining my tongue encircling each one, drawing one, then the other into my mouth. It was as if you knew, because I saw you stroke yourself, your head tossed back, eyes closed with pleasure. You encircled yourself with your own arms in sensuous delight before stretching them high above your head, lazy, preening, like a cat. You took a few steps toward the window and seemed to look straight into my eyes, but I knew you couldn't see me. You turned away and unbuttoned your skirt, kicking it aside. Then you wiggled ever so slightly as you eased your silk panties over your hips and luscious ass. You bent forward, and I caught a brief glimpse of the curls surrounding your womanhood. My cock was rigid, longing to be enveloped by the folds of your pussy. Again, you seemed to sense my presence, as you turned to face me hidden in the darkness, teasing me as you played with the wetness forming between your legs. One hand stroked your hardening nub, a finger disappearing deep inside. It could be me! So know this! Tonight, I'll **Be Watching You!** And waiting for a signal - a candle in the window - that you want me too!"

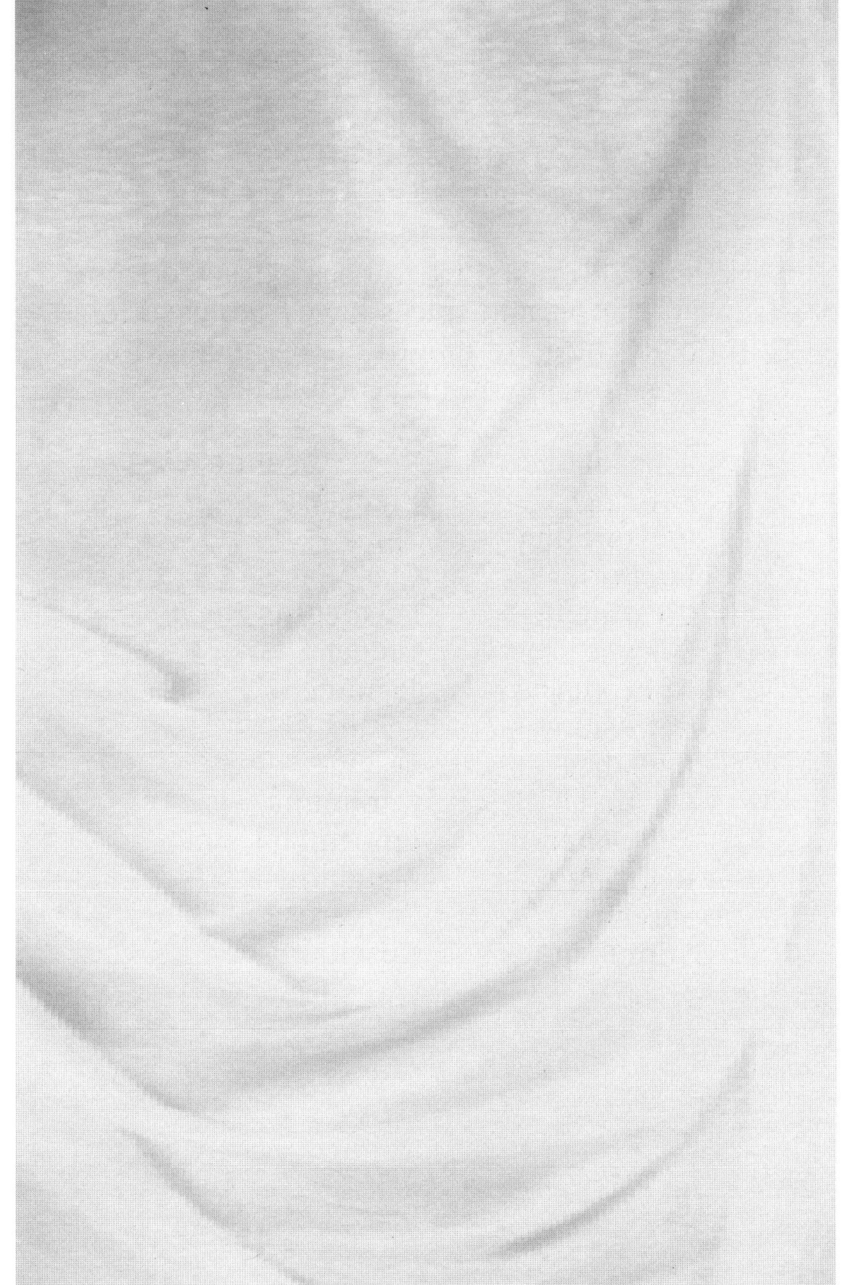

Aroma Therapy
Creating Your Mood With Scents

For over 6,000 years, fragrances extracted from flowers, herbs, and spices have been used to stimulate different moods. Experiment with just one scent, or a combination.

Sensual	Rose Absolute
Enticing	Ylang-Ylang
Invigorating	Pine
Euphoric	Clary Sage
Clearing	Eucalyptus
Spicy	Ginger
Aphrodisiac	Jasmine
Refreshing	Lemon
Radiance	Orange
Balancing	Geranium
Rejuvenating	Linden Blossom
Relaxing	Mandarin
Serenity	Palmarosa
Stimulant	Rosemary

Tell Us Your Ideas

We would greatly appreciate your taking the time to let us know your thoughts and suggestions about this book, *Naughty Games for Lovers.*

Your feedback will help us continue to find new and exciting "sexcapades" for others to enjoy.

We would also like to encourage you to submit your ideas and suggestions for other books in the "Naughty Games" series. This series will target couples at different stages in their lives and relationships.

Let us know your ideas for "sexcapades" and games you think are worth sharing with other couples in the quest for the most fulfilling relationship possible.

Please email your comments and suggestions to:

Marketing@weddingsolutionsbooks.com

Or fax us at: (619) 287-1019

Please also check out our website, www.weddingsolutionsbooks.com for more exciting titles currently available

Thank you and best wishes for a beautiful and fulfilling relationship!